The Christian Wallet

*Spending, Giving, and Living
with a Conscience*

MIKE SLAUGHTER

with Karen Perry Smith

WJK WESTMINSTER
JOHN KNOX PRESS
LOUISVILLE · KENTUCKY

First edition
Published by Westminster John Knox Press
Louisville, Kentucky

16 17 18 19 20 21 22 23 24 25—10 9 8 7 6 5 4 3 2 1

Book design by Drew Stevens
Cover design by designpointinc.com

Library of Congress Cataloging-in-Publication Data

Slaughter, Michael.
  The Christian wallet : spending, giving, and living with a conscience / Mike Slaughter ; with Karen Perry Smith.
    pages cm
  Includes bibliographical references.
  ISBN 978-0-664-26029-3 (alk. paper)
  1. Consumption (Economics)—Religious aspects—Christianity. 2. Money—Religious aspects—Christianity. 3. Finance, Personal—Religious aspects—Christianity. I. Title.
  BR115.C67S53 2016
  241'.68—dc23

                                                                2015026179

PRINTED IN THE UNITED STATES OF AMERICA

♾ The paper used in this publication meets the minimum requirements
of the American National Standard for Information Sciences—
Permanence of Paper for Printed Library Materials, ANSI Z39.48-1992.

Most Westminster John Knox Press books are available at special quantity discounts when purchased in bulk by corporations, organizations, and special-interest groups. For more information, please e-mail SpecialSales@wjkbooks.com.

In honor of my mother,
Bettye Ramage Slaughter.
Thankful for your faithfulness!

Contents

PART II. HOW WE GIVE

PART III. HOW WE LIVE

Introduction

Every Christian knows that we are called to love God with all our heart, mind, soul, and strength. But what about our wallet? We get asked to open it every Sunday when the offering basket comes by and are told that's being a "good steward." Jesus' definition of stewardship, however, is far more encompassing and radical. Almost 40 percent of his parables found in the Gospels deal with true faith and faith's relationship to our money and possessions.

Jesus' encounter with a young "ruler" (the reference to the man as a ruler identifies him as a person of status and means) dismisses any notion that a commitment to faithful discipleship can be separated from our economic lifestyle practices. When the young man asks, "What must I do to inherit eternal life?" Jesus' response doesn't allow wiggle room to define eternal life as simply a personalized faith or the practice of moral behavior. "You still lack one thing," Jesus says. "Sell everything you have and give to the poor, and you will have treasure in heaven. Then come, follow me" (Luke 18:18–22).

There is no clearer indicator of our ultimate values than our financial priorities and practices—how we spend, how we live, how we save, and how we give reveal the true altar of our hearts. In Jesus' own words, "For where your treasure is, there your heart will be also. . . . No one can serve two masters; either you'll hate the one and love the other; or you'll be devoted to one and despise the other. You cannot serve both God and money" (Matt. 6:21, 25).

We live in a commodity culture that promises happiness found in the accumulation and abundance of possessions. John Kavanaugh, in his book *Following Christ in a Consumer Society*, writes, "The pre-eminent values of the Commodity Form are producing, marketing, and consuming. These values are the ethical lenses through which we are conditioned to perceive our worth and importance."[1] He goes on to say, "Consumption, consequently, is not just an economic factor. It emerges as a 'way of life.' It is an addiction."

Writing this book has been a real challenge for me. I am not immune from the virus of consumption I describe in these pages. Like so many others, I suffer from influenza of affluence—known these days as "affluenza." I'm not going to mention how much money I spent on that pair of jeans. I would like to use the excuse that the company only uses organic cotton, pays workers a livable wage, and works to ensure safe working conditions—all very important factors in the consideration of our purchasing choices—but let's be honest, I spend too much money on clothes and purchase items that I don't need or rarely wear.

Jen Hatmaker, in her book *7: An Experimental Munity against Excess*, expresses it best:

> I could blame Big Marketing for selling me imagined needs. I could point a finger at culture for peer pressuring me into having nicer things. I might implicate modern parenting, which encourages endless purchases for the kids, ensuring they aren't the "have-nots" in a sea of "haves." I could just dismiss it all with a shrug and casual wave of the hand. Oh, you know me! Retail therapy! But if I'm being truthful, this is a sickening cycle of consumerism that I perpetuate constantly. I used to pardon excess from the tension of the gospel by saying, "Oh, it doesn't matter how much you have; it's what you do with it." But that exemption is folding in on itself lately. Plus, let's be honest: what does "it's what you do with it" even mean? Are we really doing something honorable with our stuff other than consuming it? I'm not sure carting it all off after we're bored with those particular items is a helpful response since we just replace it with more.[2]

"Sell your possessions and give to the poor. Then come and follow me." These words haunt me. I find myself wrestling with tough questions: "Am I truly a follower of Jesus or just a fan?" "Have I bought into a self-serving, consumerist, Americanized, version of the gospel? "Has growing older and having a more comfortable lifestyle dulled the edge of my commitment to follow Jesus in costly discipleship?" How we use our money is undoubtedly, unavoidably a spiritual question.

It's no secret that American Christianity is in decline. Surveys reveal that the fastest growing religion is no religion, and one speaker at a recent seminar I attended said that only 4 percent of eighteen-to-thirty-five-year-olds are actively involved in a faith community. Why has the church become irrelevant to the vast majority of Western people? I wonder if it is because we have become the modern church of Laodicea. That's the church Jesus addresses in the book of Revelation, saying, "'You say, "I am rich; I have acquired wealth and do not need a thing." But you do not realize that you are wretched, pitiful, poor, blind and naked. I counsel you to buy from me gold refined in the fire, so you can become rich; and white clothes to wear, so you can cover your shameful nakedness; and salve to put on your eyes, so you can see'" (Rev. 3:17–18).

Have we failed to recognize our own poverty in the comfort of our wealth? Jesus' parable in Mark 4 about the farmer sowing seed in four different types of soil reveals that our attitude toward money affects our receptivity to the Spirit's work in our lives. The seed that the farmer sows represents the creative Logos (Word) of God. The problem in the parable is not the quality of the seed being sown but the receptivity of the soil. All four soils receive the same quality of seed. But the health of the soil will determine the fruitfulness of the crop. Take a look at the third type of soil where promising growth begins but is then choked out: "'Other seed fell among thorns, which grew up and choked the plants, so they did not bear grain'" (v. 7). Verses 18–19 give a clearer description of the "root" problem: "'Still others, like seed sown among thorns, hear the word; but the worries of this life, the deceitfulness of wealth and the desire for other things come in and choke the word, making it unfruitful.'"

When we chase money instead of Christ's mission, we miss

the abundant life for which we were created. Our lives fail to produce a kingdom crop. In Hatmaker's words,

> The average human gets around twenty-five thousand days on this earth, and most of us in the United States of America will get a few more. That's it. This life is a breath. Heaven is coming fast, and we live in that thin space where faith and obedience have relevance. We have this one life to offer; there is no second chance, no Plan B for the good news. We get one shot at living to expand the kingdom, fighting for justice. We'll stand before Jesus once, and none of our luxuries will accompany us. We will have one moment to say, "This is how I lived."[3]

Conscientious and compassionate use of our money in a world where people spend $310 million on costumes for their pets and $5 billion on entertaining ringtones for their phones is not an easy task. The temptation to spend now and think later (or never!) is ever present, but with good intentions and prayerful hearts, we can slow down and reflect on what we earn, how we spend it, who is affected by it, and who we can share it with. Some of this reflection may lead to new questions: Should we pay more for fairly traded and ethically farmed food or spend less at the grocery so we can give more to the church's feeding ministry? What are the hidden costs of moving to a more affluent area where we are insulated from our city's poor communities? How do we make the difficult changes required to live on less?

This book asks difficult questions about morality and money, exploring the issues at play while acknowledging there are no easy answers. It is my prayer that you and I will be wrestling with these questions together, making the hard choices to transform our lifestyles, and experience true transformation in the process.

PART I

How We Spend

1

Culture of Consumerism

Southwestern Ohio is not the snowiest of climates, but we do have inconvenient snow storms that can deposit four-to-eight inches of the white stuff in our driveways a few times each year. One of our church members, another Mike, had long desired a snow blower to use to make those occasions a little easier. Recognizing that a snow blower was more of a luxury than a necessity, Mike hated to make the investment in a piece of equipment that would be hauled out of the garage a few times each winter while requiring storage and maintenance over the other three seasons. Yet with a physically demanding day job that required long and unpredictable hours, he could give some justification for the purchase.

Noting that the four neighboring homes around his also seemed to be snow blowerless, he approached the neighbors with what sounded like an excellent suggestion—purchasing a "communal" snow blower that each neighbor could in turn store, maintain, and use, splitting both the up-front purchase cost and the ongoing maintenance costs among multiple house-holds. Each neighbor he spoke with had a somewhat affirming yet half-hearted response to the plan, and no decision could ever be reached. Finally, in frustration, Mike purchased a snow blower, a piece of luxury equipment that proves extremely helpful on average two times each year while sitting useless for an additional 363 days.

After making the purchase, he generously used the blower at his own expense and effort the first winter to clear the neighbors' drives, but soon each household purchased its own. Now five snow blowers are used sporadically to complete tasks that easily could have been accomplished by one. What can I say? We Americans love our stuff! Why share when you can own your own while also ensuring that it has more horsepower and a wider snow-clearing width than the Joneses' machine next door? As Tim "the Tool Man" Taylor used to observe in Comedian Tim Allen's sitcom *Home Improvement*, there is nothing better to some homeowners than power-tool bragging rights.

The snow-blower story is one limited example of a much wider "Keeping Up with the Joneses" culture, a long-standing meme in the Western world for using one's neighbor as a comparative benchmark for success. The phrase was popularized in 1913 when cartoonist Arthur Momand created a comic strip by that title, which was distributed by Associated Newspapers. A recent television commercial for a new SUV taps perfectly into the culture of conspicuous consumption that the phrase embodies. A young couple is working in the kitchen of what appears to be a nice, upper-middle-class home when the wife spots a neighbor couple pulling into their own drive with a new vehicle and calls it to her husband's attention. The husband asks, "What did they get?" as he moves toward the window and pulls a pair of binoculars from a kitchen drawer. (Apparently, neighbor watching is a regular pastime.) The wife replies, "I don't know" while they both stare at the new vehicle wistfully for a moment. She then adds, "It's pretty nice. Maybe he got a raise." The husband responds, "Good for him." After the briefest of pauses, the wife retorts ruefully with a tinge of accusation, "Good for her." The new car owner spots them at the window, making a point to wave cheerily—perhaps rubbing a little salt in the wound of his one-upmanship victory.[1]

Hoarders, on the A&E network, is not a show I choose to watch regularly, but I can't seem to tear my eyes away from the screen if I stumble upon it while channel surfing. I am both repulsed and fascinated by how some live who have slipped into the dark underbelly of where our consumer-driven passions can carry us. I would never live like that, I protest to myself, while mentally cataloguing the mounds of baseball memorabilia (one of my main life passions in addition to Jesus) collecting dust in my basement and the plethora of leather jackets I no longer wear that crowd my closet space. Yet daily I continue to peruse persuasive e-mail offers for new coats from my favorite department store. Even my Mac's Web browser knows my tastes perfectly and helpfully displays just about every tasteful temptation I struggle to resist in the sidebar. I am a huge fan of every i-gadget that has ever been invented. Although I have never stood outside an Apple store for forty-eight hours in a line that stretches for blocks to purchase the newest release of the iPhone, I can understand why many people do. I am not immune by any means to the siren call of consumerism.

So what's wrong with consuming; what's wrong with stuff? Nothing, in and of itself. Everyone in the world must consume. Consuming keeps us alive, and it fuels our economies. The problem arises in excessive consumption, when consumption becomes harmful both to self and others and even becomes addictive. We purchase stuff in a vain effort to find life fulfillment, a fulfillment that can only be experienced in a life-transforming relationship with Jesus Christ and a commitment to serve his interest in others. Conspicuous consumption has practical consequences for both ourselves and others as well as significant moral and theological implications.

THE CONSEQUENCES OF CONSUMERISM

As individuals, our consumerist tendencies are not doing us any personal favors. As my wife, Carolyn, and I consider an eventual downsizing of our home, we already feel overwhelmed thinking about what we will do with all of the stuff collected in our basement and garage over the course of our forty-plus years of marriage. Consequences of our compulsive consumption can not only include hoarding like on that reality TV show but also unhealthy behaviors like compulsive buying disorder (CBD).

The World Psychiatric Association describes CBD as "characterized by excessive shopping cognitions and buying behavior that leads to distress or impairment."[2] The disorder exists worldwide and affects about 6 percent of the U.S. general population. CBD sufferers go through four distinct phases as they go out to pursue new purchases: (1) anticipation, (2) preparation, (3) shopping, and (4) spending. Culmination of the fourth step, however, typically results in "a sense of letdown, or disappointment with oneself" and negative emotions like depression, anxiety, boredom, and anger. Even those of us without CBD can identify with the letdown we experience after a new prized possession is in hand and then quickly becomes one more piece of "stuff" that we need to store, clean, maintain, and pay off.

This use of shopping to medicate an internal void reminds me of a line from a country music golden oldie: we are "lookin' for love in all the wrong places."[3] We will not find life significance or fulfillment in the high-end open-air shopping centers that are starting to dot our urban and suburban landscapes or via our Amazon Prime membership, convenient as it may be.

The other very painful, personal consequence of our culture of consumerism is debt. In 2005, for the first time since the Great Depression, Americans developed a negative savings rate. Consumers spent all that they earned and then some, pushing the personal savings rate 0.5 percent into negative territory.[4]

The "Great Recession" that started in 2008 gave many consumers a badly needed wake-up call, and many began to focus on paying off debts and avoiding new ones. *Businessweek* magazine recently reported that American household debt hit its peak in 2007 and has since fallen 15 percent.[5] But, the article goes on to state, "Home mortgage debt accounted for much of the decline—it's dropped 22 percent since 2007. Consumer debt, on the other hand, has continued to increase and just reached an all-time high of $3.2 trillion."

In preparation for this book and a related sermon series I preached, we at Ginghamsburg Church conducted a survey about people's money habits and opinions. Five hundred and sixty-four people responded, the majority of whom are between the ages of thirty and sixty—the prime years of our earning and spending. More than two-thirds of our respondents reported carrying debt other than a mortgage. Of those with such debts, 54 percent are in debt to their credit-card companies.

The average household's credit-card debt in the United States as of fall 2014 was close to $7,000. Marketwatch.com reported that consumers are rapidly reaching the "credit card debt 'tipping point,' where minimum payments become unsustainable and delinquencies skyrocket."[6] However, the $7,000-per-household figure does not tell the full story. That is the number derived when all U.S. households are apportioned an equal amount of the national credit-card debt load. If only those households actually carrying credit-card debt are taken into consideration, the average household debt is $15,252.[7]

In our survey, 50 percent of respondents carried over $20,000 in nonmortgage debt. Debt is never our friend. It is not only a fiscal issue but also a spiritual one. Proverbs 22:7 reminds us, "The rich rule over the poor, and the borrower is slave to the lender." Verses 26–27 add, "Do not be one who shakes hands in pledge or puts up security for debts; if you lack the means to pay, your very bed will be snatched from under you." The apostle Paul reminds us in Romans 13:8: "Let no debt remain outstanding, except the continuing debt to love one another, for whoever loves others has fulfilled the law." Debt is a form of slavery; we are both enslaved to our debtors and enslaved to our pasts. We are working today for what we consumed yesterday instead of living expectantly and dreaming new God dreams for tomorrow.

If you are caught in a whirlpool of debt (or maybe cesspool

would be a better analogy), I recommend that you seek help now. Many families at Ginghamsburg Church have found financial freedom and peace through debt counseling and excellent programs like Financial Peace University. Dealing with debt starts like any other form of recovery: claim it, own it, and then do something about it. Ignoring debt totals and avoiding collectors' calls is a very short-term, stress-inducing, and ineffective strategy. God's call is for us to be investors in God's economic priorities. We are not designed to be simply consumers of stuff, trapped by the debt that fuels it, but to be producers of God's blessings into the lives of others. Don't let shame or negative, self-fulfilling prophecies stop you from dealing with debt. The only real shame is found in failing to take action to do something about it.

MORE THAN OUR FAIR SHARE

Rampant consumerism is also a sin in God's economy because we become selfish takers and terrible givers. After Cain murders his brother Abel in the book of Genesis and God inquires as to Abel's whereabouts, Cain snippily replies, "I don't know. Am I my brother's keeper?" (Gen. 4:9). God does not directly answer the rhetorical question but makes it blatantly clear that the only acceptable response is "Yes!" Cain faces harsh consequences for failing to practice God's directive.

I suspect most of us are guilty as well. We may not be "murdering" anyone with our own hands, but we are unfairly consuming the majority of the world's resources and in turn littering it with the majority of its trash. We ignore global (and local) inequalities of wealth and opportunity, turning a blind, uncaring eye to the suffering, oppressed, and lost. According to the 2014 Human Development Report issued by the United Nations, 1.2 billion people attempt to live on less than $1.25 per day.[8] Their poverty is accompanied by additional deprivations, including lowered health, education, and living

standards. I found one statistic in that report simply amazing—the eighty-five wealthiest people in the world have the
combined equivalent wealth of the 3.5 billion poorest people
on the planet. A recent report from Oxfam International indicated that 50 percent of the world's wealth will be held by the
richest 1 percent of the population by 2016.[9] As Pope Francis noted, "Human rights are violated not only by terrorism,
repression or assassination, but also by unfair economic structures that create huge inequalities."[10]

The U.N. report goes on to state that nearly 2.2 billion people, nearly a third of earth's population, are living in poverty.
Nearly half of all workers, more than 1.5 billion, are in "infor-
mal or precarious employment." Eight hundred and forty-two
million are chronically hungry. Ninety-two percent of children
live in developing countries, where 50 out of 100 "will not
have their birth registered, 68 will not receive early childhood
education . . . and [the growth of] 30 will be stunted. . . . Close
to 156 million children are stunted, a result of undernutrition
and infection." These are sobering statistics, especially when
one considers how we merrily spend $804.42 per family on
just our holiday shopping.[11]

While 842 million are hungry, the U.S. Center for Disease
Control reports that more than one-third of Americans are
obese, with the estimated annual medical costs associated with
obesity boasting a $147 billion price tag. This $147 billion
could easily put 842 million children, women, and men out
of harm's way.[12] God's heart must break, both for the hungry
and for those of us suffering the unhealthy consequences of our
overeating and our processed-food diets, such as heart disease,
stroke, type 2 diabetes, and certain types of cancer.

One day we will also answer to God as to why we allowed
our rampant materialism to ruin the beautiful planet God created. The Worldwatch Institute reports that the United States
represents less than 5 percent of the global population while
using about a quarter of the world's fossil-fuel resources.[13] Each
day the United States consumes on average 18.5 million barrels

of oil. China comes in second at nearly 10 million barrels per day[14] (despite the fact that China has more than four times the U.S. population.)[15] The 203 countries at the bottom of the consumption ranking use less than 500 barrels per day.[16]

The use of these fossil fuels, of course, for electricity, industry, and transportation is also a primary contributor to the carbon footprint, representing approximately 58 percent of global greenhouse gas emissions. The United States contributes 19 percent of the world's global emissions while once again only hosting 5 percent of the world's population.[17]

In 2012 Americans generated about 251 million tons of trash, representing 4.38 pounds per person per day.[18] Consumer packaging from the many products we buy has accounted for more than 20 percent of all U.S. landfill waste over the last two decades. This type of consumption, and the resulting pollution, is not sustainable. It has to stop. Money can't buy us love, and neither can our stuff.

Christians, especially those who might self-identify as "conservative evangelical," are often not known for their support of environmental issues. If asked, "Is God green?" many of them might answer, "No," followed by "Isn't God going to destroy the earth someday anyway? Didn't God give us all of this stuff for our good and our pleasure?"

Frankly, I cannot help but see God's concern for all of creation throughout Scripture. Seven times in the story of earth's creation found in Genesis 1, we see God create, step back admiringly, and declare it "good." The story culminates in verse 31: "God saw all that he had made, and it was very good." I am pretty sure "all" in the original Hebrew means "all." The world is not bad; it is just broken—broken by the same sin that set humankind apart from God, requiring the reconciliation of the cross.

I also read in my Bible that God designed us to be caretakers, not careless consumers. Some have argued that God set us up as creation's masters to do with it as we see fit. They may even cite verse 26 from Genesis 1 to make their case: "Then

God said, 'Let us make humankind in our image, in our likeness, so that they may rule over the fish in the sea and the birds
in the sky, over the livestock and all the wild animals, and over
all the creatures that move along the ground.'" So the question
at hand is, "What does 'rule' mean?" As always when I read
the Old Testament, I must view Scripture through the lens of
Jesus, who told his disciples, "'You know that those who are
regarded as rulers of the Gentiles lord it over them, and their
high officials exercise authority over them. Not so with you.
Instead, whoever wants to become great among you must be
your servant, and whoever wants to be first must be slave of
all. For even the Son of Man did not come to be served, but
to serve, and to give his life as a ransom for many'" (Mark
10:42–45). To rule in Jesus' kingdom is to serve—not to ruin
with selfish intent.

That God is simply going to destroy the world anyway
is also not what I read in my Bible. Isaiah 61:2–4, the passage I always note as being Jesus' mission statement (see Luke
4:17–19), indicates that in the "year of the LORD's favor," the
redeemed poor, brokenhearted, captives, and prisoners will
"rebuild the ancient ruins and restore the places long devas-
tated; they will renew the ruined cities that have been devas-
tated for generations." Note all the "re" words—God is not
starting over from scratch! We will return to this theme of how
environmental consciousness should inform our consuming
decisions in chapter 3.

CONSUMING OUR TIME AND ENERGY

Not only does our slavish devotion to materialism create waste
materials; it also leads to the wasting of our short allotment of
time on planet earth. Moments we could use to have an actual
face-to-face conversation with our spouse or play *HORSE* in
the driveway with our soon-to-leave-home son or daughter are
redirected toward taking care of stuff. Garages need cleaning

out; lawns need mowing; bric-a-brac needs dusting; oil needs changing;, closets and drawers are bulging at the seams—and the list goes on. Our stuff reduces the quantity and quality of our time for investment into key relationships. Large houses mean we can spend an entire evening at home and never encounter another family member. Or if we are in the same room, Junior is texting on the latest smartphone, the spouse is shopping on the tablet, and you're engrossed in a mindless TV show. We build a wrap-around front porch on the new and bigger house but never sit outside at dusk to greet the neighbors. Life is short, and soon we're dead. It's time to haul out the trite but oh-so-painfully true platitude—"You can't take it with you."

Jesus made it crystal clear in Matthew 6 that we cannot serve both God and money; we cannot serve both God and stuff. Jesus said, "'Therefore I tell you, do not worry about your life, what you will eat or drink; or about your body, what you will wear. Is not life more important than food, and the body more important than clothes?'" (v. 25). The key is in verse 33: "'But seek first his kingdom, and his righteousness, and all these things will be given to you as well.'" In other words, don't chase the stuff; chase the mission. If your eye is healthy and focused on the mission, the money and what it needs to purchase will follow.

Worry is another key word within Jesus' verse 25 directive. Our worry reveals our places of greatest devotion, and too often that place of worry is finances. I meet many people from within my own congregation who are making every effort to be faithful Jesus followers yet find themselves derailed by fears and worries surrounding their money matters. Whenever I preach a financial series at Ginghamsburg, I hear from attendees about their financial troubles and weaknesses. During the last series, one young man candidly shared with me that he struggles with this "trusting in Jesus" issue. "I love my family and my kids, but I am going to have to figure out how to afford college for them some day. I would love to spend more time with them while they are young but have to be focused on chasing the money while I can. Otherwise, it isn't going to happen. I want to ensure they have all of the stuff my own parents were unable to afford for me when I was growing up." Another man, who is closer to retirement age, confessed that he lies awake at nights worrying about his net worth and how to live comfortably after retirement. He wants to ensure that his family is "financially secure." On the surface, it is an important goal. I can relate! However, it becomes a problem when our first priority is building net worth and we start neglecting soul worth.

Ironically, for many people, the greater their wealth, the greater their worry. In 2011, Boston College's Center on Wealth and Philanthropy posted the results of a four-year study of the wealthy that was funded in part by the Gates Foundation. As part of the study, one hundred and sixty-five households with an average net worth of $78 million responded to a survey, with two of the respondents being billionaires. Graeme Wood's article "The Secrets of the Super-Rich" in *The Atlantic* summarizes the results, which concluded the following:

> The respondents turn out to be a generally dissatisfied lot, whose money has contributed to deep anxieties involving love, work, and family. Indeed, they are frequently dissatisfied even with their sizable fortunes. Most of them still do not consider themselves financially secure; for that, they say, they would require on average one-quarter more wealth than they currently possess. (Remember: this is a population with assets in the tens of millions of dollars and above.) One respondent, the heir to an enormous fortune, says that what matters most to him is his Christianity, and that his greatest aspiration is "to love the Lord, my family, and my friends." He also reports that he wouldn't feel financially secure until he had $1 billion in the bank.[19]

No wonder Jesus declared, "'It is easier for a camel to go through the eye of a needle than for someone who is rich to enter the kingdom of God'" (Matt. 19:24).

Wood goes on to report, "A vast body of psychological evidence shows that the pleasures of consumption wear off through time and depend heavily on one's frame of reference. . . . In the case of the very wealthy, such forms of consumption can become so commonplace as to lose all psychological benefit: constant luxury is, in a sense, no luxury at all."

Two of the Boston College survey's architects noted that eventually "most wealthy people discover the satisfactions of philanthropy." The experience of giving money away "in addition to being powerful and empowering, also helps teach that money sometimes carries a burden with it." I would like to strengthen that supposition and proclaim that money *always* carries a burden with it. We are our sister's and brother's keeper! And, as a wise man of God also once pointed out, "It is more blessed to give than to receive" (Acts 20:35). Bill and Melinda Gates and their friend Warren Buffett are key examples of the super wealthy who have confirmed that truth.

As Jesus told the rich young ruler, "'If you want to be perfect, go, sell your possessions and give to the poor, and you will have treasure in heaven. Then come, follow me'" (Matt. 19:21). The word *perfect* in the Greek is *telos*, which means to be fully made complete—to become perfect just as God is perfect. We see in Jesus in the flesh the picture of what we are to become. In this completeness we discover restored humanity.

But the action step for becoming perfect is just a little too painful for me to fathom in my selfish desire for bigger, better, and more—"'Sell your possessions and give to the poor.'" God says to me as I read these words, "Mike, you need to simplify. You have way too much stuff in your life. It's weighing you down; it's holding you back." The poor, as Scripture reveals repeatedly, are the very heart and priority of God. More than two thousand Bible verses speak to God's justice for the poor. We are crazy to ignore that in our lifestyles of conspicuous consumption.

"'Give to the poor, and you will have treasure in heaven. Then come, follow me'" (Matt. 19:21). Note the order of the directive: (1) "'Give to the poor'"; (2) then, "'come, follow me.'" Have I been deluding myself? Am I a Jesus fan or a follower? "When the young man heard this, he went away sad because he had great wealth" (v. 22). That's one response. Now, what will I do with this directive? What will you?

I don't believe that Jesus literally wants us to give away everything we own, have, or enjoy. If I give away all that I have, I can no longer be a source of health, healing, or blessing in the lives of others. But I do believe he is calling us to gut-check and spirit-check our fiscal priorities. What we do from this point forward with our Christian wallets matters. We must start spending, giving, and living with the conscience of Christ.

QUESTIONS FOR REFLECTION

- In what ways does your "stuff" cause you anxiety or otherwise diminish your quality of life?
- What kinds of debt do you carry? How did that situation develop?

Meet Jason Byram

Jason, age forty-one, is an investment realtor who handles both commercial and residential properties. Jason also manages a team of medical insurance professionals. He and his wife Sarah have the joy and challenge of sharing a combined four sons and three daughters, ranging from age eight to nineteen, in their often busy, bustling household. However, Jason recently made a startling claim: "Being broke has brought me happiness"—not a sentiment many of us would likely embrace. Jason himself never would have made such a proclamation when I officiated his marriage to Sarah less than five years ago.

The wedding was held at the new home that Jason and

Sarah had bought to start their life together, and it was beautiful—a 5,500-square-foot, open-floor-plan home that was one of the nicest houses in the entire village of Tipp City, a fairly affluent white-collar bedroom community just north of Dayton, where Ginghamsburg Church is located.

Jason reminisced with me how he and Sarah, both ambitious salespeople, had sat in the driveway one day just before moving in saying, "Can you believe we did this?" They had a sense of wonder at what the work of their hands had enabled them to achieve. For some reason, Jason now remarks incredulously, "Our attitude was all about us. We wanted to show everyone that we had made it. In retrospect, I have no idea why that felt so important to us at the time."

The "good times" were not to last. Within a short period of time, family finances began to shift—and not for the better. The impending implementation of the Affordable Care Act affected Jason's medical insurance business, leading to a significant loss of income. At the same time, Sarah was forced to switch career paths. The Byrams now make $100,000 less a year than they did in 2009 before their personal financial downturn. Jason could no longer take pleasure in their large beautiful home, which also featured a $900-per-month electric bill. Instead of being a blessing, the house had become an excessive burden.

There is good news, however. Jason and Sarah did not bury their heads in the sand but soberly assessed the new reality and began to make changes. Jason took Financial Peace University via the church, and I asked him what his key takeaways were from the experience. First, Jason said, both the curriculum and the good people he met through the program helped him to see that he had to stop making his life all about making money. He took a long, hard look at all of the household dollars that were going out the door, and he and Sarah set a new budget and committed to living within their means and paying off debt. Jason knew that living more simply would someday position him also to give more. He looked at the big "dream house" with new eyes, surprised to note that what had once made him feel good would now leave him sick to his stomach. "A place that size could house twenty to thirty people, and I had been using it for a single family."

Jason also began to sell "everything that wasn't attached to the house," including cars and motorcycles. He used the proceeds to pay off every debt he could so that the family could securely live within the new, reduced budget. He and the family then downsized into a more modest home—and didn't look back.

This experience would not typically make someone as cheerful as Jason, so I had to ask him about that. He said, "I am so much happier now. I am more frugal in the right ways with my money, always asking, 'Do I really need this?' before making a purchase. I also started giving money away. I love passing on a $20 bill to the guy down the street if he needs it. I even started tithing across multiple ministries, even though on the surface it didn't seem to make sense. I couldn't really afford it if you just looked at the numbers on paper." Jason explained that when he was initially struggling with the tithing concept, he heard God's almost audible voice saying, "Trust me, Jason." At first Jason fearfully responded, "God, I don't know how to give you this and have a cheerful heart about it. But, I will be obedient until I become cheerful." Now, Jason says, he has been so converted in his attitude that he would fear not tithing.

Jason's life today isn't perfect. He says God is still testing him. God does not provide an overabundance, despite Jason's new obedience and generosity. "Each year," Jason says, "for one reason or another our income has continued to decline. I will just finish paying off a $2,000 debt and something will break requiring $2,000 for repair. It is almost like clockwork. I am still at the point where God is teaching me. Whenever I finally get it down, God will bless me with abundance. Until then, God knows I am only too likely to use it all up on myself." Jason jokes that he used to pray for abundance. Then his prayer switched to "Just get me out of this mess." Now, it has become "God, give me exactly what I need," and God does.

Spiritual growth has not been the only win. Jason enjoys no longer being a slave to his stuff. "Even when I had tons of money, my stuff owned me. Just look at the motorcycle, for example. I had to store it, maintain it, winterize it." Jason exclaims that two of his current homes could handily fit inside the old one, and everything is "much tidier and easier now."

Jason philosophically says, "It was a hard message to receive, and I never would have received it if I had not gotten such a big wake-up call. I was stubborn; I was that guy who would never listen. Now, I am more broke than I have been in a long time. I know what it means to live paycheck to paycheck. But I want to share with everyone how much happier I am. . . . Being broke has brought me happiness."

2

Balancing the Budget

One day I was idly scrolling through the newsfeed on my Yahoo phone app. There were a few of the typical Hollywood break-up stories, cute pet videos, and amazing moments in sports, but most of the feed seemed to encourage me to eat better, work on my abs, or get my money matters in order. Article titles included "Living Paycheck to Paycheck? Here's Your Solution"; "10 Unnecessary Purchases That Are Eating Up Your Budget"; and "7 Money Habits to Start Now." This wasn't too surprising. It was January, the season of New Year's resolutions. Money, health, and beauty always seem to rank highly as areas of focus just after the first of the year. Many of us love to read the articles and declare the best of intentions; however, we typically fall short in the execution. I always dread January at my gym; it's hard to find open workout machines. But by mid-February or before, availability is no longer an issue.

Frankly, setting and adhering to a budget is one of those good intentions at which most Americans are not very successful. Gallup reported survey results in June 2013 revealing that only one in three Americans prepare a detailed household budget. Gallup goes on to indicate that "those with at least some college education, conservatives, Republicans, independents, and those making $75,000 a year or more are slightly more likely to prepare a detailed household budget than are their counterparts." But the survey results were not encouraging for any given demographic.[1]

It's common sense that you can't reach a destination or hit a target that you haven't identified, and budgeting is no exception. It's not particularly astounding that we undersave, overspend, and accumulate debt. We don't have a plan for where our income will go, so we also do not track where it ends up. We just know at the end of the month or before that there never seems to be quite enough left to go around.

I do not live in your household, but I can tell you where the Bureau of Labor Statistics (BLS) says your money goes. The BLS defines a "consumer unit" as "a family, single persons living alone or sharing a household with others but who are financially independent, or two or more persons living together who share expenses." In 2013, the BLS reported that the average American consumer unit age was 50.1 years old and consisted of 2.5 people and 1.3 "earners" with 1.9 vehicles.[2] Just under 64 percent are homeowners and have an average income of $63,784 before taxes. The average annual spending of the consumer unit is $51,100. That total is typically spent by dollar amount and percentage as follows:

Transportation	$9,004	17.6%
Food	$6,602	12.9%
Personal Insurance & Pensions	$5,528	10.8%
Apparel & Services	$1,604	3.1%
Entertainment	$2,482	4.9%
Housing	$17,148	33.6%
Cash Contributions	$1,834	3.6%
Health care	$3,631	7.1%
Other Expenditures	$3,267	6.4%

The "Other Expenditures" category represents "alcoholic beverages, education, miscellaneous, personal care products, reading, and tobacco products." Some of these are primarily luxury purchases, "nice to have" versus "need to have," with the exclusion of important education expenses and undoubtedly some of the personal care items. I would never encourage you to forego antiperspirant as a quick fix for bringing your spending under control.

The two highest spends were for housing and transportation, which would not surprise most adults. The third highest spend was for food. We must eat to live. Having a food budget is a nonnegotiable. However, the BLS notes that nearly 40 percent of our food purchases are for "away from home" snacks and meals. The *Christian Wallet* survey we conducted revealed that this is a stumbling block for many people: 50 percent of our respondents said that "dining out" was the area in which they are most likely to overspend. It was the most common response to that question, ahead of "things for the kids" at 25 percent and "items for the home" at 17 percent. The frenetic pace of our twenty-first-century American lifestyles, where we use the craziness of our calendars as bragging rights over our friends, makes it easy to justify the quick cruise by the fast-food drive-through window after the final soccer practice of the night wraps up. However, the effect on our health as well as our wallets is a steep price to pay for no longer allowing margins in our lives for preparing and eating a meal at home with the family.

I can preach on it, but I have also failed at it. About ten years ago when my wife, Carolyn, and I were already empty nesters, Carolyn approached me flustered after sitting down for a checkup on family finances. I remember her waving a sheet of paper in front of my face and urgently saying, "Do you know we are spending $400 a month on eating out?" We didn't even have the excuse any longer of having children in the home with crazy church, sport, and school activities to coordinate. It is so easy to slip up and stop paying attention out of convenience and busyness. Carolyn has been an incredible steward of our family finances through the years, and she made sure that trend halted abruptly and we went back on track.

Many of us have an Achilles heel where we are most likely to overspend. In my life, I have two primary places of temptation: Apple products and my wardrobe. I like nice clothes. Ginghamsburg Church is a largely blue-collar worshiping community, and on any given weekend I typically preach in a pair of jeans (accompanied by flip flops in the summer). However, I have to confess that some of those sitting in the congregation would not easily identify with the price tag that was attached to those jeans when I purchased them. Still, Carolyn and I have always done our best to live into God's plan for our money matters. In return, God has blessed us to be able to give above the tithe to the church as well as support other non-profits, missionaries, and scholarships for teens in at-risk communities. We have budgeted and tracked expenditures since the early days of our marriage, avoided most debt other than mortgage debt (now paid off), and invested significantly in saving toward the future. Yet I don't have all of my broken, materialistic money matters fixed just yet; I remain a work in progress.

The BLS cash-contributions category reflects charitable giving and giving to churches, synagogues, mosques, and other religious organizations. According to the BLS, if you look simply at giving to churches and religious organizations, the average amount of the typical consumer unit's charitable contribution was $699, a 4.8 percent drop from the previous year. In 2013, the year represented by the BLS data, *Relevant Magazine* reported, based on a Barna survey, the following statistics:

- Tithers make up only 10–25 percent of a normal congregation.
- Only 5 percent of the U.S. population tithes, with 80 percent of Americans only giving 2 percent of their income.
- Christians are only giving at 2.5 percent per capita, while during the Great Depression they gave at a 3.3 percent rate.[3]

This is not encouraging news for those of us who consider our-selves Jesus followers, keen to understand and live into the pri-orities of God for our money. We will look more at "How We Give" in part 2 of this book.

WHERE DOES YOUR MONEY GO?

Do you know how much you can afford to spend each month on eating out, new clothes, or entertainment? At the end of the month can you account for each dollar spent? According to Gallup, more than two-thirds of us can't.[4] The first, best practice for a Christian wallet is budgeting.

There are many tools available for starting and maintaining a personal budget, ranging from free online tools to software packages with various levels of features. If you do not already have a system for planning and monitoring your cash flow, I urge you to do some research and find a program you think you can stick with.

To get a basic picture of your income and outflow, grab a calculator and your most recent bank and credit-card state-ments, and fill out the "Actual" column in the chart on the following pages. Income is fairly straightforward, while the way you record expenses may vary depending on your personal habits and situation. I've left a few blank lines for things you may need to add: "Kids' stuff," for example, or maybe you spend so much on music downloads that it requires its own line item!

Subtract your total monthly expenses from your total monthly income, and what do you have left? Hopefully, there is something left that you can put away for emergencies and long-term savings. Unexpected medical bills and other crises can easily put families under financially. And even planned expenses like vacations and holiday spending can get out of control if we haven't set a budget and put money aside for these things.

If your expenses are higher than your income, giving you a

INCOME (Your monthly take-home pay and that of your spouse or other earners in the household, any other income from pension, etc.)		
EXPENSES CATEGORY	ACTUAL	BUDGETED
HOUSING (Mortgage or rent payments)		
UTILITIES (Electricity, water, phone, Internet, etc.)		
MEDICAL (Health-insurance premiums, co-pays, prescription costs, etc.)		
GROCERIES (Food you prepare at home. Can also include personal-care items or other things you purchase at a grocery store.)		
DINING OUT (Restaurants, fast food, coffee shops, etc.)		
CLOTHING (Include all family members here, or create a separate line for kids. Include dry cleaning here as well.)		
TRANSPORTATION (Gasoline, car maintenance, and/or public transportation)		
ENTERTAINMENT (Movies, media subscriptions, books, hobby supplies, etc.)		

MISCELLANEOUS (Haircuts, repair services, household items, etc.)		
GIVING (Tithes and offerings to church, donations to other organizations)		
REGULAR PAYMENTS (Monthly payments not included in any above category: car payments, gym membership, student-loan payments, credit- card fees and interest payments, day-care tuition, etc.)		
TOTAL EXPENSES		

ACTUAL INCOME: $_____

ACTUAL EXPENSES: – $_____

END-OF-MONTH BALANCE   = $_____

negative number in your "Balance" line, something definitely needs to change. Which categories of expenses were higher than you expected? Which do you have the power to lower? Clothing and entertainment purchases, for example, can be reduced with a bit of will power. Utilities and transportation, on the other hand, might not have much wiggle room, though monitoring your thermostat and choosing public transportation could help lower those expenses somewhat.

With the insights you glean from this exercise, go back and experiment with the "Budgeted" column of the chart. What amounts would need to change to bring your budget into balance?

YOUR BUDGET AS A
MORAL DOCUMENT

So far we have examined the whys and hows of budgeting from a primarily practical perspective. But this book is called *The Christian Wallet*, and not simply *The Wallet*, for a reason. What we do with our money matters to God. At the core, our relationship with money and how we spend, save, and give are deeply spiritual issues. Remember, almost 40 percent of Jesus' parables within the Gospels illustrate how faith should inform what we do with our money and possessions.

In Matthew 6, Jesus said, "'Do not store up for yourself treasures on earth, where moth and rust destroy, and where thieves break in and steal. But store up for yourselves treasures in heaven, where moth and rust do not destroy, and where thieves do not break in and steal. For where your treasure is, there your heart will be also. The eye is the lamp of the body. If your eyes are healthy, your whole body will be full of light'" (vv. 19–22). The Greek word for *healthy* used in this passage implies two connotations: clarity of focus (or single focus) and generosity. Jesus continued, "'But if your eyes are unhealthy, your whole body will be full of darkness. If then the light within you is darkness, how great is that darkness! No one can serve two masters. Either you'll hate the one and love the other, or you'll be devoted to one and despise the other. You cannot serve both God and money'" (vv. 23–24).

The major two currencies we have to spend on planet earth are time and money, and what we do with each is very revealing. I make sure to review this at least once each year in my own life, typically when I am preparing to teach our annual financial matters worship series at Ginghamsburg. The flow of my resources is the truest indicator of *what* I worship and *whom* I worship.

One great way to check your priorities is to look at your calendar for the past twelve months. What have you been spending your time on? Who have you been spending it with? Look at your budget in the same way. What do you spend your money on? Who benefits most from this spending? If you say your kids are the most important thing in your life, but every Saturday is spent on the golf course and all your disposable income goes toward new clubs and greens fees, your actions may be speaking louder than your words.

So when we claim to be followers of Jesus, why is money so important? We are to honor God in every area of our lives, and "every" means our wallets are not exempt. If you have come to that place where you have declared that Jesus is the Lord of your life, then Jesus has ultimate authority over every dimension. In Philippians 3, the apostle Paul ends his letter to the believers in Philippi with a caution and encouragement:

> Many live as enemies of the cross of Christ. Their destiny is destruction, their god is their stomach, and their glory is in their shame. Their mind is set on earthly things. But our citizenship is in heaven. And we eagerly await a Savior from there, the Lord Jesus Christ, who, by the power that enables him to bring everything under his control, will transform our lowly bodies so that they will be like his glorious body.
>
> (Phil. 3:18–21)

Enemies of Christ as described by Paul are concerned only with their own egos and appetites; they are not to serve as our role models. As Christ followers, we are now citizens of heaven awaiting the return of the King, a chosen people who are being transformed into the likeness of Christ. You and I may exist within economic and political systems, but as citizens of heaven we are not to hold the values of those earthly systems. Regardless of whether we are surrounded by capitalism, socialism, or a mixed economic model, we are to hold and demonstrate the values of the kingdom of God. Your budget is as much a moral document as any personal statement of faith you could write. Do the numbers on that chart or in your bank statement profess the values of God's kingdom or of your own earthly appetites?

Another of Jesus' parables about money is in Luke 16, when Jesus tells the disciples about a rich man whose manager was accused of wasting his resources. The manager then made special arrangements with the rich man's debtors in an attempt to save his skin. Although the actions he took were questionable, he did act shrewdly, and the rich man commended him for his shrewdness. Jesus then continued: "'Whoever can be trusted with very little can also be trusted with much, and whoever is dishonest with very little will also be dishonest with much. So if you have not been trustworthy in handling worldly wealth, who will trust you with true riches? And if you have not been trustworthy with someone else's property, who will give you property of your own?'" (vv. 10–12). As Jesus finished, the Pharisees "who loved money," started sneering at Jesus. Jesus responded, "'You are the ones who justify yourselves in the eyes of others, but God knows your hearts. What people value highly is detestable in God's sight'" (v. 15).

Of course, in the parable the rich man, the ultimate owner of all resources is God. The manager is us, all who proclaim Jesus as Lord and are entrusted by God to be wise stewards of his abundant resources. When the appetites and desires of the worldly systems consume our lives, when those values hold mastery over all of our spending decisions, then we are loving money and not God. Jesus is unequivocal—we can't serve both. And, if God knew the Pharisees' hearts, as Jesus warned, God certainly knows ours.

Each time we prepare to spend money, there are three questions we must ask ourselves:

1. Why am I spending?
2. Whose money is it that I am spending?
3. What are God's priorities in my spending?
   (We will focus on this question in chap. 3: "Conscious Spending.")

Why Am I Spending?

Why do we spend? First, we all do have real and valid needs: food, shelter, health care, clothing, and transportation are among the key essentials. Of course, just because we know them to be essential for us, we often forget how essential they are for others who are not like us. Many times we deride the homeless or impoverished, ascribing their condition to laziness or lack of initiative. In some cases people are simply stuck. You can't keep a job if you have no way to get there. This is one reason why Ginghamsburg Church is part of a ministry called Rides to Work. For three hours each morning and three hours each evening a servant picks up employed homeless people in our community and transports them to work and back. People need transportation to get to work, make a living, and support their families.

Although we may fail to recognize the needs of others who don't live like we do, we have the opposite problem when it comes to ourselves. And I am often guilty. Our tendency is to confuse imagined needs with real needs. The prophet Isaiah cautions us,

> Why spend money on what is not bread,
>   and your labor on what does not satisfy?

Listen, listen to me, and eat what is good,
and you will delight in the richest of fare."
                                        (Isaiah 55:2)

Jesus warned repeatedly, "'Watch out! Be on your guard against
all kinds of greed; life does not consist in an abundance of possessions'" (Luke 12:15).

Jesus was prescient even for the twenty-first century in his
admonition to keep one's guard up. If I have been "window
shopping" online, the next time I open Facebook, the retailer
whose site or product I had perused repeatedly shows up as a
sponsored ad on my newsfeed, sometimes with a tailored ad
featuring the exact product I had been looking at. The next
time I perform a search on Google, the search-results page
jumps in on the action as well.

As I have shared, I am an Apple fan. I have three generations
of iPods, have been through three or four different MacBooks
and MacBook Airs, and currently carry the next-to-newest version of the iPhone. It was fortunate that I was preparing to
teach a stewardship series at the church when the latest iPhone
was released, or I would have been an early, albeit unnecessary,
adopter of that as well. Why is it that we always want the next
new thing, the bigger, the better, the best? We allow ourselves
to be sucked into the consumerism vortex and can soon convince ourselves that almost all of our wants are needs. We live
in a crazy world in interesting times. Americans spend $370
million a year on pet costumes.[5] We spend $5 billion a year on
entertaining ringtones.[6] Perhaps ringtones and pet costumes
are not your area of weakness, but I suspect you could name
something that is, something that may very well be considered
as foolish in the eyes of others as a dog dressed like a princess
for Halloween seems to you.

The prophet Jeremiah referenced these intoxicating substitutes in our lives, our sinful tendency to confuse real needs
with imagined needs. God said to Jeremiah in lamenting the
unfaithfulness of God's people,

"My people have committed two sins:
They have forsaken me,
the spring of living water,
and have dug their own cisterns,
broken cisterns that cannot hold water."

(Jer. 2:13)

Jesus in turn makes plain what the spring of living water represents as he speaks to the Samaritan woman during their encounter at a well: "'Everyone who drinks this water will be thirsty again, but whoever drinks the water I give them will never thirst. Indeed, the water I give them will become in them a spring of water welling up to eternal life'" (John 4:13–14). Later, he declares, "'Let anyone who is thirsty come to me and drink. Whoever believes in me, as Scripture has said, rivers of living water will flow from within them'" (John 7:37–38). We keep drinking from the wrong well, wondering why we are never really satiated, and puzzled by, in some cases, how the debts keep piling up.

At times the wrong well may be expansive and expensive, like an extravagantly oversized home or a luxuriously equipped SUV. In many cases however, our intoxicating substitutes may be as inexpensive as a ringtone, but with repetitive spending or inefficiencies, the receipts are racked up. In my research, I found several lists identifying top ways Americans waste money.[7] Many of the wasteful areas identified were on multiple lists. Let's take a look at some of those.

Wasted Energy

One source estimated that we collectively throw away $443 billion on avoidable energy costs. So unplugging energy vampires when not in use, turning off lights once in a while, and setting our thermostats at more reasonable ranges can add up. If I start to complain about being chilly in the winter when Carolyn turns the thermostat down, she gently reminds me how fortunate we are to have a furnace at all and to have drawers full of sweaters to put on.

Daily Coffee Trips

One survey indicated that American workers who regularly buy coffee out each week spend on average $1,092 annually. That's $21 a week, or approximately four-to-five fancy coffee drinks. What else could you do with that money? My United Methodist denomination's "Imagine No Malaria" initiative has the goal of eliminating death by malaria in Africa in our lifetime. Each $10 contributed provides one insecticide-treated bed net, and $1,092 would buy 109 nets, potentially protecting more than three hundred lives. Three hundred lives or three hundred lattes? I can brew at home.

Premium Cable Packages

If I think I can actually justify the exorbitant costs of premium packages against the quantity of my television viewing time, I am simply watching too much TV—end of discussion.

Unused Gym Memberships

When gyms set sales targets for their membership fees, they do so based on the expectation that only 18 percent of gym members will show up consistently to work out. That's in part why it's so much easier to find workout machines available in mid-February than in mid-January. The other 82 percent of gym members are no longer showing up.

ATM Fees

When we use out-of-network ATM machines to withdraw cash, we typically pay between $3 to $4 per use. Planning ahead could eliminate this.

Unhealthy Habits

Americans spend $117 billion on fast food each year, and $2.8 billion on Halloween candy, just to name a few of our bad-health habits. Other costly culprits include alcohol, tobacco, and soda (or pop, as it's known in my part of the country).

Unused Gift Cards

Approximately $2 billion worth of gift cards go unredeemed each year. I recently opened up the glove compartment of our car and found several tucked inside among the extra napkins and vehicle manuals.

Credit-Card Interest

Collectively, Americans owe over $800 billion in credit-card debt. If credit-card interest rates average between 13 to 15 percent, and many are higher, you don't actually have to do the math to know that the interest charges are astronomical.

Whose Money Am I Spending?

As we identified in the Luke 16 parable about the rich man and the shrewd manager, God is the owner of all of the resources of the universe, no matter what we treat solely as our own. We smile when we read "The Toddler's Creed," attributed to Dr. Burton White, that starts out,

> If it's mine, it's mine;
> if it's yours, it's mine;
> if I like it, it's mine;
> if I can take it from you, it is mine;
> if I am playing with something,
>   *all* of the pieces are mine;
> if I think it is mine, it is.[8]

Yet that is often our own attitude toward God's resources that have been entrusted into our care. We forget that God is the source and supplier of every dollar, talent, and piece of property that comes into our hands. Scripture is quite clear:

> The earth is the LORD's, and everything in it,
> the world, and all who live in it.
>
> (Ps. 24:1)

> To the LORD your God belong the heavens, even
> the highest heavens, the earth and everything in it.
>
> (Deut. 10:14)

> "The earth is the Lord's, and everything in it."
>
> (1 Cor. 10:26)

Note that the word "everything" appears in each of these examples.

Look at Deuteronomy 8:10–18, when Moses is sharing God's law with the Israelites, who have been wandering in the desert following their miraculous escape from Egypt.

> When you have eaten and are satisfied, praise the LORD your God for the good land he has given you. Be careful that you do not forget the LORD your God, failing to observe his commands, his laws and his decrees that I am giving you this day. Otherwise, when you eat and are satisfied, when you build fine houses and settle down, and when your herds and flocks grow large and your silver and gold increase and all you have is multiplied, then your heart will become proud and you will forget the LORD your God, who brought you out of Egypt, out of the land of slavery. He led you through the vast and dreadful wilderness, that thirsty and waterless land, with its venomous snakes and scorpions. He brought you water out of hard rock. He gave you manna to eat in the wilderness, something your ancestors had never known, to humble and test you so that in

the end it might go well with you. You may say to yourself, "My power and the strength of my hands have produced this wealth for me." But remember the LORD your God, for it is he who gives you the ability to produce wealth, and so confirms his covenant, which he swore to your ancestors, as it is today.

This passage first reminds us of the importance of gratitude. It is hard to be cognizant of the material and spiritual blessings God provides daily without an attitude of gratitude. We are next cautioned to obey God's commands, which include God's clear directives on the priority of the poor, widowed, and orphaned. The passage repeatedly stresses that God is the source of all that we have and all that is accomplished: *he* led; *he* brought; *he* gave. Yet in our arrogance, we make it all about us. We become consumers instead of stewards or managers of all of God's provided resources.

Whose money is it that we are spending? The answer seems clear.

TACKLING DEBT

In chapter 3 we will more closely examine God's priorities in our spending. But developing and adhering to a budget that reflects a Christian wallet is an essential first step. Many of us are not starting our budgeting journey with a clean slate. As we noted in chapter 1, the average household with unsecured debt has over $15,000 in credit-card debt alone.[9] Debt may be a very real presence in your life and has to be taken into consideration as you map out your money matters.

Denial is not a solution for debt resolution. For years, Carolyn and I worked toward the goal of "D-Day," the day that we would finally be debt free, including from mortgages. In 2014, we did it; D-Day arrived. In January 2014 we finished off the mortgage on our home. It felt great.

I encourage you also to know when your D-Day will be

by sitting down, making an accurate accounting of everything you owe, and then putting together (or revisiting) your plan to accomplish it. For many of us, mortgage debt is the last to go and the hardest to finish. All debt is regrettable, but most of us are not in the position to pay cash for a house, although up-front cash, or at least a hefty down payment, should always be the preference. The other debts to be eliminated include other forms of secured debts, with car loans being a prime example. They are unlikely to serve as an itemized deduction on your income tax and are typically "secured" by items that depreciate in value. If you have a car loan, pay it off as quickly as possible. Then consider setting that same amount aside once the debt is gone until you have enough money to buy your next *used* vehicle with cash. Debt does not honor God.

Of course, credit cards are the riskiest and usually most expensive form of debt. However, an increasing debt problem for young Americans is student-loan debt. As I taught our most recent financial series at Ginghamsburg, the local newspaper shared these depressing statistics: "Aggregate student loan debt exceeds $1 trillion (about $200 billion more than Americans owe in credit-card debt) and students are adding to that at a rate of $100 billion per year." It goes on to state, "Several million student loan borrowers are in default, and student loan debt is second only to mortgage debt for 29- to 37-year olds."[10] These are seriously scary statistics, and I believe that the underlying problems are bigger than anything you and I can resolve on our own. However, we can help our children minimize their debt load.

1. Open a 529 savings plan. According to the IRS, the major advantage of a 529 plan is that "earnings are not subject to federal tax and generally not subject to state tax when used for the qualified education expenses of the designated beneficiary, such as tuition, fees, books, as well as room and board."[11]

2. Assess with your child if a community college, which is typically much more affordable, might offer a

shorter-term two-year program that will match with the child's future professional interests. If not, your student may still be able to complete the first two years of a four-year degree at a community college.

3. Seek help. Go to seminars, talk to advisors, pursue wise counsel. Ensure you and your child are pursuing the right avenues and not leaving available non-debt sources of funding on the table.

4. Do not empower your child to make foolish decisions. Jon Hlavac, a certified financial planner who assists our church employees with retirement planning and volunteers his time to teach financial classes for us, reminds parents, "You don't give your eighteen-year-old carte blanche to go out and spend $100,000 on anything else. Why would you let them make a solo or ill-advised decision about where to go to college?" Our children have dreams, and our natural desire as parents is to make them come true, but we mustn't let them mortgage their futures to pay off the past.

5. The best rule of thumb I have heard is this: If your student is pursuing a career in which the opening annual salary might reasonably be expected to be in the $30,000 range, then don't let the college debt, if he or she must take it on, exceed $30,000. The debt you borrow for college should never exceed what you think you will earn your first year, assuming you can find employment.

Once you have an unobstructed view of all the debts you owe, you can start to take positive action. The best method of debt elimination is not to acquire it in the first place, something a budget will help you achieve.

There are varying strategies for paying off existing debt. Two popular ones are the avalanche approach and the snowball approach. The avalanche approach recommends that you order your debts from highest interest rate to lowest. Then send all available extra cash to the debt with the highest interest rate regardless of its outstanding balance while you continue to make minimum payments on all other debts. Once that debt is paid off, then apply that payment amount and all available cash to the next highest interest debt. (Note that you may need to reorder the original list because variable interest rates may change over time.) Relentlessly keep at this until all debts, both short- and long-term, are paid. The snowball technique is similar, only you order your pay-off by debt balance instead of interest rates. The first debt to pay off would be the one with the lowest outstanding balance, and then on up the list. The theory behind the snowball technique is that achieving victories more quickly in debt reduction will keep you better motivated for the long haul.

My best advice is to seek training or help. Financial Peace University, Crown Financial Ministries, and other ministries local churches may offer can be truly transformational. I have seen families even with the most significant and seemingly insurmountable debt loads eliminate that debt in five to eight years. There is hope.

A popular mantra in project management is "Plan the work, and work the plan." Debt can be highly oppressive and emotional. It may keep you up nights; you may feel shame. But the same mantra can and will work. I am not an expert on debt, but I do know that we serve a God with cattle on a thousand hillsides, and debt is *not* God's plan for your life (Ps. 50:10).

QUESTIONS FOR REFLECTION

- Did anything surprise you as you filled out the budget chart in this chapter? What does your spending say about what you value?
- What steps do you need to take to balance your budget in accordance with your income and values?

Meet the Osenkos

Brandon and Dawn Osenko are forty-one-year-old married professionals with two children, ages five and seven. Brandon works as an engineer in the automotive industry, and Dawn is a registered nurse. I first became familiar with the Osenko family when they competed in and won a special financial competition at Ginghamsburg Church dubbed the Race to Freedom, modeled loosely after a similar competition hosted by an area credit union. Three couples were chosen to compete over the course of the year after submitting a detailed application. On being selected, each couple was assigned a professional financial coach who would work with them for several months to help them master their money matters. At the end, the family that had made the most positive strides forward in making and maintaining a budget, increasing savings, conquering debt, and reaching the tithe would win.

Why did the Osenkos see the need to compete? About five years prior, Brandon and Dawn had been living comfortably but largely paycheck to paycheck. They had some debt, but Brandon was employed with a good salary, Dawn was attending nursing school, and life felt doable. Then, as so often happens when we are least prepared, the perfect storm began to brew. First, while Dawn was in her final year of nursing school, Brandon changed jobs to a position located four hours south of their current location. Because the family did not want to be separated and did not have relatives in the new location for Brandon to bunk with until the northern home sold, they purchased a new house and began the interesting challenge of paying two mortgages simultaneously. Of course, the timing turned out to be terrible. The mortgage banking crisis was breaking, the recession was beginning, and their hopes of selling their previous home rapidly became a pipe dream. They soon took out a home line of credit just to make ends meet.

They added a second child to the family, which multiplied child-care costs. The new company Brandon worked for declared bankruptcy, and the fear and debt started to mount. Brandon and Dawn knew they needed a solution and took Ginghamsburg's "Get Out of Debt for Good" class as well as entered Financial Peace University. They also took "their books," so to speak, in to meet with our chief financial officer Nate Gibson, an MBA and CPA, who they hoped would have all of the answers. As Dawn indicated, they were eager to receive a magical answer that would make all of their troubles go away. Nate looked at the numbers and said, "This can't work." He was the one who invited and encouraged them to enter the "Race to Freedom."

One of Ginghamsburg's volunteer financial counselors was assigned as their coach. The coach, along with the tools that the Osenkos had acquired in Financial Peace University, helped them put together a budget. Brandon started using an Excel spreadsheet to track the budget to their spending and their bank account balance back to both. Brandon describes it as a somewhat cumbersome tool but helpful for knowing where their money was going and what to project based on previous years. Their financial counselor helped them analyze their spending and shopping habits to identify waste and areas for reduction. The Osenkos quickly learned that one of their pricey pitfalls was the convenience of fast food and eating out. Brandon travels extensively, both Brandon and Dawn work, there are two kids to manage, and meals at home are tough. The counselor encouraged them to "stop the bleeding." They reviewed better ways to grocery shop, plan meals ahead of time, use the crockpot, and ensure more dinners at home. Dawn said, "Our coach was not afraid to call us on our stuff. She took a look at what we were spending on restaurants and said, 'Guys, this is ridiculous.'"

She also counseled them on how to handle the actual task of bill paying. Her suggestions included going through the mail as they brought it in the door, discarding the junk, and placing those items that needed processing in a designated location until bill-paying time. Previously their modus operandi had been to pile all of the mail on a desk and ignore it (and the stress it might induce) for as long as possible.

They did not take all of their financial counselor's suggestions, and she would acquiesce after they made their case. A prime example was day-care costs. The Osenkos were appreciative of the care their children were receiving at the church's preschool and child-care program, despite the $960 per month price tag. The counselor felt they could save money by pursuing a different option, but Dawn and Brandon had their own cost-benefit analysis using the equation "Value equals benefit minus cost," and felt the care and training their children received was well worth it.

The financial counselor and the Osenkos also worked on significant debt reduction and savings strategies. The debts started to be paid off. Brandon had signed up for a flexible spending account that would allow them to set aside pre-tax dollars to pay for child care, thereby reducing their taxable income. When the reimbursements rolled in for child-care fees that had already been paid, those flex-plan dollars were put toward debt instead—just one creative strategy for paying down debt. Brandon described it as a type of "forced savings account."

During the race competition, the Osenkos attended Financial Peace University for a second time to reinforce what they had learned previously, and he also took a Crown Financial class, which helped them more firmly connect the dots between their money and God's intent. Because of the race and new financial practices, the Osenkos were able to pay off over $30,000 in debt, save $8,000, tighten household spending to match the budget, and reach a more-than-biblical tithe of 12 percent.

The race wrapped up more than a year ago, and I asked the Osenkos how they are doing. They confessed that eating out is still a weakness, and their debt reduction has become a little more lackluster. The previous year was tough because Dawn had to make a job change that resulted in reduction to part-time. They recently experienced a furnace emergency, and the house's roof had to be replaced. However, they are grateful that their emergency savings came through. "Prior to the race," Brandon said, "we would have resorted to credit to cover those urgencies." It's now a new year, and the Osenkos are resolved to put those areas of slippage back on track.

Brandon said, "A budget is a process, not an end goal. It has to evolve and change as life changes."

I then asked for their advice to other couples that are financially struggling and fearful. Dawn offered, "If it doesn't work out the first time around, don't give up. Learn from the failures; keep moving forward." Both encouraged people not to let their pride stand in the way and to seek help. Said Dawn, "Accept the fear, and do it anyway."

3

Conscious Spending

In the summer of 2013, I was invited to teach a group of United Methodist pastors in Ho Chi Minh City in Vietnam. While there, I eagerly took advantage of Vietnam's reputation for fine tailors who were skilled at making custom-fit clothing at far less cost than you would ever find in the United States. I visited a small, local tailor's shop and ordered a silk suit for the astoundingly low price of only $200. I returned to the shop four times for fittings and adjustments and left with a final product that fit me far better than any off-the-rack suit ever could. The shop itself was a storefront only; the actual labor was completed at an alternative site. When I would show for a fitting, a man would simply ride up on a motorbike, suit in hand. I left the shop after the final visit a very happy customer. I had purchased a high-end-quality product with only a small outlay of cash.

Fast-forward two years when I wore that now-favorite suit to church one day rather than my typical jeans and flip-flops to conduct a funeral. Later that day, I shared the suit's origin and low price with a young staff member. I was drawn up short when she noted, "For that price, you have to wonder if the suit was made by child laborers or in some unsafe or unhealthy environment." The truth was, I didn't know. I had praised the fit and loved the cost, but it had never occurred to me that my purchase could have easily underwritten unsafe or unjust labor practices. How many of us always just look for "a great deal" without asking the critical questions about the true costs inflicted on health, safety, or the environment during the product's production?

In the last chapter, we focused on two of the three questions we must learn to ask ourselves when we prepare to spend money from our Christian wallets: (1) Why am I spending? and (2) Whose money is it that I am spending? Now let's turn to the third key question: What are God's priorities in my spending?

The survey we conducted indicates that Christians may not typically spend much time on this question before making purchases. The survey asked how often, when shopping, respondents take into consideration the price, environmental impact, impact on the local economy, wages/treatment of workers, and their own family's health and wellness. The majority of respondents claim to be price conscious and somewhat concerned about the family's health, but the other considerations did not fare so well:

Purchase consideration	% who always/almost always consider it
Price	75.0
Environment	5.6
Local economy	5.6
Wages & treatment of workers	4.8
Health & wellness of the family	30.8

Now, price is an important factor, especially when we are attempting to live within the carefully defined and tracked budget we talked about in chapter 2. However, it can't be the only factor and may very well be trumped by other priorities within God's economy. Let's first look at the health and wellness of our family, which often hinges on what we put into our bodies.

HEALTH AND WELLNESS

I believe as a Jesus follower that we have only one new birth but many conversions. One of my conversions was about my own health and a renewed commitment to maintaining the only body I will ever have. By the time I was in my early forties, my body fat was 34 percent. Although a person would not have looked at me and identified me as obese, I had developed a paunch and clearly was not fit. Then a heart scare when I was forty-nine gave me the real wake-up call. I was eating out with Carolyn and other family members in Cincinnati when I suddenly collapsed onto Carolyn's lap. A squad was called, and the paramedic reported that my heart was arrhythmic and my blood pressure had dropped to 60 over 40. I was rushed to a nearby hospital where I fortunately recovered. But I clearly needed to make some changes in my life, and quickly. I had jeopardized the only hands, feet, and voice that I had to live out God's calling.

I sought out a trainer, changed my diet, and announced my plans to the congregation. It helps to have over three thousand people holding you accountable for life change. In my mid-sixties, I now run up to four miles a few times each week and spend time at the gym building strength and flexibility. I eat right (with the exception of giving in to my favorite— ice cream—a few times each year). I have more energy than I had in my forties. The gym membership and healthier foods cost more than no membership and junk food, but the "value equals benefits minus cost" equation clearly weighs in on the side of taking care of myself. Carolyn also practices healthy eating and exercise habits.

My daughter Kristen is a dietician at a children's hospital in Cincinnati and recently brought to my attention that diabetes rates among children are skyrocketing. A study in the *Journal of the American Medical Association* reported, "The prevalence of diabetes in children shot up dramatically between 2000 and 2009. . . . The prevalence of type 2 diabetes—which is associated with obesity—jumped more than 30% in the same period."[1] The *Christian Wallet* survey indicated that many of us tend to overspend on eating out, and that no doubt contributes to these statistics—especially the fast food we cram into our children many week nights as we scramble among lessons, practices, and performances. Thirty-five percent said they overspend on groceries, which could be a result of buying more expensive organic products and other health food but could also very well be a result of carts piled high with processed snacks and dessert foods that pad our grocery bill and our waistlines without offering any real nutritional value.

Consider these findings from the U.S. Department of Agriculture:

> Americans are consuming more calories per day than they did 40 years ago. In 1970, Americans consumed an estimated 2,109 calories per person per day; whereas in 2010, they consumed an estimated 2,568 calories (after adjusting for plate waste, spoilage, and other food losses). Of this 459-calorie increase, grains (mainly refined grains) accounted for 180 calories; added fats & oils, 225 calories; added sugar & sweeteners, 21 calories; dairy fats, 19 calories; fruits and vegetables, 12 calories; and meats, eggs, and nuts, 16 calories. Only dairy products declined (13 calories) during the time period."[2]

The report also notes that we consume more than the recommended amounts of meat and grains but eat less than the recommended amounts of fruit, vegetables, and dairy. Yes, we can blame the McDonalds and other fast food restaurants of the world for the problem (and they no doubt do have some culpability), but how many of us teach our children to select the apples as their Happy Meal side dish instead of the fries? And why wouldn't Junior want fries just like Dad?

This is not an eating-and-exercise book, but God does prioritize our health and our children's health and expects us to spend wisely from our Christian wallets in this area. In addition, God expects us to take into consideration how our eating choices impact the world around us. Americans are wasteful when it comes to food. Each year we waste 141 trillion calories worth of food, which amounts to 133 billion pounds. That's 1,249 calories per capita each day. This includes food that became spoiled, discarded by retailers because of blemishes, or that was left on our plates.[3]

The damning information does not stop there. A USDA Economic Research Service report published in February, 2014, states that "according to the U.S. Environmental Protection Agency (EPA), food waste accounted for 34 million tons (almost 14 percent) out of the 250 million tons of municipal solid waste in the United States in 2010 as measured before recycling (EPA, 2011). Less than 3 percent of this food waste was recovered and recycled, with the remainder going to landfills or incinerators."[4] I remember one evening when I was visiting family in Boston sitting inside a restaurant located next to where earlier in the day an open-air street market had sold mounds of produce. Once the market ended, bulldozers came in to smash and remove the unsold leftovers.

This kind of waste is certainly an environmental issue, but it is also an economic and human rights one. The USDA report goes on to conclude, "If food loss is prevented or reduced to the extent that less food is needed to feed people (i.e., the demand for food decreases), then this would likely reduce food prices in the United States and the rest of the world."[5] As we noted in chapter 1, 842 million children, women, and men in the world are chronically hungry.[6] Our garbage disposals, a typically American household appliance, "eat" better than most of the world eats, as do our pets.

Food is among the most necessary things on which we spend

our money, but its necessity for our survival does not negate our responsibility to spend that money (which is really God's money, remember?) in ways that do not harm our planet, our bodies, and the bodies of the world's most vulnerable people.

ENVIRONMENTAL CONCERNS

The *Christian Wallet* survey results indicated that only 4.6 percent of respondents take environmental impacts into consideration when making purchasing decisions. As we discovered in chapter 1, God expresses concern for creation throughout Scripture. In Leviticus 25, he gives the Israelites very careful instructions as to how they are to use the land: "When you enter the land I am going to give you, the land itself must observe a sabbath to the LORD. For six years sow your fields, and for six years prune your vineyards and gather their crops. But in the seventh year the land is to have a year of sabbath rest, a sabbath to the LORD. Do not sow your fields or prune your vineyards" (Lev. 25:2–4).

We read in Psalm 96 that God invites creation into a kingdom celebration:

> Let the heavens rejoice, let the earth be glad;
>   let the sea resound, and all that is in it.
> Let the fields be jubilant, and everything in them;
>   let all the trees of the forest sing for joy.
> Let all creation rejoice before the LORD, for he comes,
> he comes to judge the earth.
>   (Ps. 96:11–13)

Hosea 4 reveals what happens when we fail to follow God's directives on how we are to live within the land:

> The LORD has a charge to bring
>   against you who live in the land:

"There is no faithfulness, no love,
no acknowledgment of God in the land.
. . . .
Because of this the land dries up,
    and all who live in it waste away;
the beasts of the field, the birds in the sky
    and the fish in the sea are swept away.
                          (Hos. 4:1, 3)

The earth matters to God, and God's people have a responsibility to the earth. We are our brothers' and sisters' keepers, and we are to tend God's garden. But while we argue over the scientific evidence of climate change, a recent study in *Science* warned that our oceans are facing a major extinction event because of the rise in global temperatures. *Time* magazine, which reported on the study, pointed out that "coral reefs are dying, fish stocks are collapsing, seas are acidifying, and surviving species are migrating to cleaner, cooler waters wherever they can find them."[7]

Our wastefulness and disregard for the consequences of our consumption are having a real impact on the health of our planet. From the oil we use to make our ubiquitous plastic products and to transport everything (plastic or not, including ourselves) from here to there, to the disposable packaging everything comes in, the cycle of consumption and waste is embedded in the most mundane things of our daily lives. But there are ways to break this cycle.

In "Good Stuff? A Behind-the-Scenes Guide to the Things We Buy," the Worldwatch Institute offers some practical tips on what they have labeled as the principles of good consumption.[8] Suggestions include the following:

- Reduce. Reuse. Recycle.
- Stay close to home—shorten commutes, eat locally, shop nearby.
- Minimize the use of the car—walk, bike, take public transportation.

- Use your shopping choices to enforce good behavior within private industry; use your voting choices to enforce good behavior by government.
- Prioritize purchases, and think hard about your choices for big energy-guzzling items like refrigerators.
- Enjoy what you have—the things that are yours alone and the things that belong to all of us—like water, air, and green spaces.

Carolyn and I are conscientious about the plastics we purchase and use and make a point to recycle everything we can. On garbage collection day, our recycle bins far exceed our bags (or I should say, bag) of garbage. It has become for us a commitment and lifestyle, not just a once-in-a-while feel-good thing. I confess, however, that I have been focused on environmentally responsible consumption decisions much more than I have been on the ethical treatment of workers, at least before starting this project.

FAIR TRADE

Our *Christian Wallet* survey revealed that less than 5 percent of the respondents always or almost always take the wages and treatment of the workers who produce the goods we purchase into consideration when shopping. But God reveals in the Word how he feels about the ethical treatment of workers. In Isaiah 58, God notes to the prophet Isaiah that the people of Israel are complaining that God has been ignoring them. They are puzzled: "'Why have we fasted,' they say, 'and you have not seen it? Why have we humbled ourselves, and you have not noticed?'" (Isa. 58:3). To paraphrase, "But God, we have been going through all of the right religious rituals! Why are you ignoring us?" God immediately responds in the remainder of verse 3, "Yet on the day of your fasting, you do as you please and exploit all your workers."

As I confessed regarding my Vietnamese suit, I have also been lax in paying attention to the conditions and pay of those who make affordable products I enjoy. I can become indignant when the media splashes a tragic story across the airwaves and Internet about a new incident of child slavery or underpaid workers in unsafe spaces being killed in preventable fires and building collapses. Typically, however, it is easier for me, like most people, to stay in my safe consumerist cocoon. We look at price; we look at quality; and we buy. The hands and lives of those who made our purchase possible seldom merit a fleeting thought. God says, "You cannot fast as you do today and expect your voice to be heard on high" (Isa. 58:4). I am working on this.

As a young pastor, I was fortunate to be among other young pastors like Rick Warren of Saddleback Church in which a group of businesspersons chose to invest by providing business training and exposure. Pastors are well equipped in seminaries on theology, preaching, and pastoral care but receive little practical knowledge or experience in leading an organization. As part of this training, we visited some of the top companies in the country at the time. One of those visits was to Harley-Davidson, where we met with the senior executives and learned more about what it means to build brand loyalty. Harley-Davidson is a master at building a following of passionate people who are willing to spend money on almost anything branded with the Harley-Davidson name. As one executive pointed out, "You don't see people tattooing 'Honda' to their bodies." Harley's branding strategy is crucial to the company's success because it is in the branding success that Harley makes its profits. We learned that the motorcycles themselves were costly to produce and had a small profit margin as a result. The company really made its money on branded shirts, jewelry, cups, décor, and leathers. The clothing segment of the business was significant. As executives shared at the time, "We can have a shirt made in China for $3 and sell it in the U.S. for $39."

I used to own a Harley motorcycle after saving for ten years to purchase it with cash. I have since sold it, choosing to move on to new pursuits and time with the grandkids. However, I still own Harley attire and was recently inspired to pull out some of the items tucked away in my closet. The first item I grabbed was a leather motorcycle jacket. Harley-Davidson, of course, promotes itself as an American company. One of its successful taglines has been "American by birth. Rebel by choice." The tag inside the jacket read, "An American Icon/ Made in China." When I purchased the jacket for $500, I never checked that tag, much less asked myself or anyone else questions about how much the Chinese laborers who produced it had been paid or under what conditions they were working. Yet questions like that are an important part of what it means to spend with a conscience.

The unethical treatment of workers is a global issue and sadly produces many of the products stuffed in our closets and garages. The International Labour Organization (ILO) estimates that "20.9 million people are victims of forced labor globally, trapped in jobs into which they were coerced or deceived and which they cannot leave." Of those, 11.4 million are women and girls, and 5.5 million are children. The Asia-Pacific region hosts 56 percent of the victims, and 18.7 million are "exploited in the private economy by individuals or enterprises."[9] Yes, slavery is alive and well in the world.

Child labor on the aggregate is much greater even than simply those who are considered "forced labor." On average, one in every seven children in the world can be classified as a child laborer.[10]

Even when laborers are not forced to work, many work within unsafe conditions with deplorable consequences. The United Nations reports that "every year approximately 337 million people are victims of work accidents, and more than 2.3 million people die from occupational injuries or work-related diseases."[11] Those are big numbers, and we tend to find some sort of odd self-absolution within the many zeros that follow the first few digits. It's almost like we believe the numbers are so large that we are inadequate to do anything about them. But we need to remember that each victim is someone's spouse, parent, or child, and God has numbered the hairs on each of their heads.

It's also easy to say, "That's in Indonesia or China, and what can I possibly do about that?" However, 12 million undocumented immigrants work in the United States, and many of those are highly underpaid and heavily exploited by their employers.[12] The U.S. State Department admitted that human trafficking and forced labor is an issue in the United States in a June 2014 statement: "The United States is a source, transit, and destination country for men, women, and children—both U.S. citizens and foreign nationals—subjected to sex trafficking and forced labor, including domestic servitude."[13] Some of that trafficking is directed toward manufacturing services.

Many American companies benefit, at least indirectly if not directly, from the unethical treatment of workers in our increasingly globalized economy. Using cheap labor (i.e., underpaid workers both here and abroad) is a major way many retailers keep prices "low" for us while maximizing corporate profits. Some of the suppliers who comprise our favorite retail outlets' global supply chains have horrific records of abusive labor practices, sometimes with devastating results. In May 2015, dozens of people died in a fire at a rubber-slipper factory in Manila, Philippines. One man who lost family members in the disaster reported that second-floor windows in the building were covered with iron grills that prevented escape.[14] Previously, in April 2013, a factory building called Rana Plaza, that had previously been deemed unsafe by officials although without any follow-up, collapsed in Bangladesh, killing at least 142 workers and injuring more than a thousand more. Walmart was one of several companies for which the factory produced clothing.[15]

Sadly, Rana Plaza was not the first incident where more than a hundred Bangladeshi workers had been killed in a single incident because of safety violations. Bangladesh has become the world's second-leading garment exporter next to China, with the lowest labor costs in the world. The minimum wage for

garment workers is set at $37 per month, two dollars less than
the Harley-Davidson price for the one shirt I previously mentioned. In total, Bangladesh has more than five thousand clothing factories employing a total of 3.2 million workers. Most
major clothing companies have benefited from their services
in addition to Walmart, including Sears, Gap, and Tommy
Hilfiger.[16] Any of those sound familiar?

Walmart has certainly not been alone in benefiting from the
unethical treatment of workers. Their size simply makes them
more visible. Even that most beloved of American companies,
Disney, has not been immune. Reportedly, a Chinese factory
that produces Disney books employs children as young as age
fourteen to work six or seven day weeks for 33 to 41 cents per
hour.[17] This is a far cry from the lavish reception our own children receive when we visit a Disney theme park.

If you are like me, this feels very heavy. What truly can we
do about it? I think the first objective is to begin to educate
ourselves. Go to the websites of your favorite retailers, and see
if and how they address corporate social-responsibility policies
and supplier enforcement. If you aren't satisfied with what you
see, vote with your voice (or e-mail) and wallet. Develop a sense
of your own role and responsibility for egregious employment
practices. Go to www.slaveryfootprint.org, and take a survey
that calculates approximately how many slaves you are personally using to stock your pantry and closet.

The Institute for Humane Education has published five
tips for keeping a sweatshop-free closet: "buy less"; "go used";
"make your own"; "check labels"; and "research companies."

Buy Less

Ever run out of hangers before you run out of clean laundry
to hang up? Many of us have far more clothing items than we
need. I would also add an addendum to the "Buy less" tip:
"Don't replace it until you have to." As I've shared, I love
my Apple products. Keeping up with the latest and greatest

technology makes me feel good, and technology companies are only too happy to satisfy my craving. New and improved devices roll out like clockwork, and planned obsolescence can be a real factor.

But we don't have to succumb to it. Baratunde Thurston recently wrote a commentary for *Fast Company* magazine called "Hopping Off the New-Device Treadmill." He described how he struggles with the "Theory of Device Relativity," which "holds that as phones of those around you grow in size, yours shrinks in stature." But Baratunde has decided to hang onto his existing model saying he has an "increasingly inescapable sense that if I get a new phone just because I can, I am accelerating the suffering of the people who make them."[18]

A U.N. study published in 2013 predicted that "e-waste" (electronic waste) would grow to 65.4 million metric tons by 2017, "the weight equivalent of 200 Empire State Buildings or 11 Great Pyramids of Giza." That's a 25 percent increase in e-waste quantity from 2012.[19]

Go Used

When we purchase from a gently used resale store, we are reducing demand for new products and typically keeping our money within the local economy and/or serving a good cause. Ginghamsburg Church has three gently used clothing, furniture, and décor outlets with proceeds serving our outreach missions.

Make Your Own

Making things on one's own may be easiest for the more creative or handy among us, but remember, there is a YouTube video out there for almost anything you may ever want to attempt. Everything from home décor to toothpaste can be made at home at a greatly reduced cost and impact on global workers and the environment.

Check Labels

Labels may indicate that an item is "sweatshop free" or fair trade. "Fair trade" is a social movement dedicated to helping product producers, typically individuals or small groups of people in developing countries, acquire a fair price for their products. The goal of the movement is to reduce poverty for those producing the goods, ensure the ethical treatment of workers and farmers, and promote practices that are environmentally friendly and sustainable. Two of Ginghamsburg's gently used retail outlets carry fair-trade products onsite along with their resale items. Carolyn and I like to buy our fair-trade coffee and chocolates there and have also purchased some beautiful gifts, including a pair of earrings this past Christmas for my daughter-in-law. Learn more about fair trade at www.fairtrade.net.

Research Companies

Responsible companies are often happy to shout their fair practices from the rooftops (or their websites), but it can be harder to learn what goes on behind the scenes at some of the largest and most profitable companies. Organizations like Green America offer searchable databases of products and companies to report on dangerous or questionable practices. Visit www
.greenamerica.org/programs/responsibleshopper/.

The ethical treatment of all of God's children is a significantly complex issue and not one that is easily resolved. But, we have to start by recognizing our own culpability and collusion. We can no longer use an "ignorance is bliss" defense as an out for our careless use of the Christian wallet.

BUYING LOCAL

Although I have paid close attention to how my food selections impact my health over the past decade and have tried to avoid wastefulness with what I buy and use, I have not always been as cognizant about how my consumption habits have affected others. One key way that I am working to reform my own consumer habits in this area is shopping locally. In other words, what I can buy from a local vendor, I will. I also make a concerted effort to patronize locally based restaurants when possible instead of always heading to the nearest familiar chain.

Studies have shown that buying local keeps more money in the local economy—68 cents of every dollar as compared to 43 cents spent at a national chain.[20] The New Economics Foundation found that buying food at a farmer's market or CSA keeps twice as much money in the local economy.[21] In addition to supporting your own neighbors and the economic health of your community, buying local is a great way to improve your consumption habits in all the other ways we've discussed in this chapter.

The Michigan State University Extension Office describes the health benefits of eating locally. With less time between harvest and table, our fresh foods tend to have more flavor; they are not shipped across the country for several days in refrigerated trucks. Anyone who has eaten a local-market or backyard tomato versus a formerly refrigerated variety from the grocery store chain will immediately know what I am talking about. Local food is often healthier with more nutrients. A Ginghamsburg Church member a few years ago was inspired to start Food from the Earth on our Tipp City campus property. It is a one-acre, biointensive, organic vegetable garden that provides its shareholders and Ginghamsburg's two food pantries with freshly harvested produce throughout the summer—a win-win both for the investors and those who may be unable to afford fresh produce otherwise.

Buying local also benefits the environment by avoiding the pollution caused by shipping products cross-country or even across continents in some cases. Supporting local farms and gardens helps ensure green space in your community, and the food should be safer because you can ask, investigate, and know how it has been handled, and you can find out how the workers who grew the food were treated or supported.

While locally owned retailers may still sell products made with unethical, sweatshop labor (you'll still want to check the records of your favorite brands), these smaller businesses are often more likely to feature specialty products that are locally made and/or fairly traded. The United States has a long way to go in ensuring a fair minimum wage that people can actually support their families on, but small businesses, whose owners know their workers personally and care about their well-being, may be more likely to be voluntarily paying a higher wage to their hourly employees.

GLOBAL CONSCIOUSNESS

Companies are becoming increasingly aware of what it means to be good corporate citizens. This positive trajectory, however, will only continue if consumers make positive global citizenry an important issue and use the weight of their purchasing power to enforce it. I have seen encouraging signs, as demonstrated by two companies recently profiled in *Fast Company*, one of my favorite magazines. Chipotle's CEO Steve Ells founded Chipotle over twenty years ago with a focus on fresh ingredients that "evolved over time into an awareness of all of the forms of exploitation inherent in traditional fast food— of animals and the environment and even of the customers." The profile indicates that Chipotle emphasizes social goals over financial performance.[22]

When Danielle Sacks interviewed Rose Marcario, president and CEO of outdoor-clothing retailer Patagonia, Marcario talked about the company's well-known "Don't Buy This" campaign. The company founder's "very basic philosophy has always been to make the very best product, make it as durable as possible."[23] Marcario went on to explain that the marketing mantra "not to buy" is really saying, "'Don't buy more than what you need.' The more you consume, the more strain it has on the earth's resources. We don't want that because we all care about this nest we're in." She also discussed the durability of their products, indicating that they can be handed down from generation to generation. A consumer can "bring it back to us, and we'll repair it." This is a great example of capitalism with a conscience.

Our consumerism impacts many things all around the world, but no effect may be more devastating than the impact on the health of our own family relationships. Isaiah 5:8 reads,

> Woe to you who add house to house
>   and join field to field
> till no space is left
>   and you live alone in the land.

Our consuming habits have left no margins in our lives. We are either buying stuff, cleaning stuff, maintaining stuff, or working to pay it off. We are caught up in the never-ending chase for the almighty dollar. Our time is completely consumed. Yet it is in the margins of our lives that our closest relationships are formed. When we commit to the discipline of living more simply, we have more time and energy to invest in those who are most important to us. We won't mourn the busted snow blower, our work desk, or our favorite restaurant as we approach death. We will either celebrate, or regret, our key relationships.

QUESTIONS FOR REFLECTION

- Are you willing to pay more for a product to ensure that the workers who made it are being paid and treated fairly, or that the product is not damaging to your health or the health of the planet?
- What is one change you can commit to making that would improve the moral impact of your purchasing?

Meet Shannon Sampley

Shannon Sampley knows how to stretch a dollar. She is thirty-six, single, and employed as an office administrator with a modest income. Shannon described her childhood economic background as working class. "I never felt poor," she said, "but was very aware of my parents' need to work." Family vacations were rare, and Shannon missed out on some of the material luxuries enjoyed by her school peers. But she never felt deprived.

Money was not a regular topic of discussion in the Sampley household. Shannon's best indicator for knowing when funds were especially tight was when the family was unable to afford pizza after church, typically a weekly tradition. Because finances were not discussed with the children, she did not learn much about budgeting or balancing a checkbook. That knowledge would be won through the "school of hard knocks," as Shannon ruefully described it.

At the age of eighteen, Shannon left home and completed one year of college. After deciding not to return for her sophomore year, she started working as a live-in nanny. After leaving that position, she moved out on her own and worked as a "day nanny" for two additional households. "I wish I had appreciated at the time how good I had it as a 'live-in' for that first year," Shannon laughed as we discussed it. "My only out-of-pocket expenses were a car payment, auto insurance, and health insurance. Once I moved out on my own, things got pretty tight. Reality hit." A nanny's pay kept her fed and housed but little else. "I accumulated car, medical, and credit-card debt. I felt stuck and was tired of never getting ahead," she told me.

Determined to get herself "unstuck" financially, Shannon took Financial Peace University at our church. Within four-teen months, she was able to pay off all of her debt. "I did not make more money during that time," she said, "but I learned how to manage what I did have. Finally, I had some-one, a mentor, who could walk me through budgeting and saving, not just surviving but planning ahead." Shannon was so inspired by her own experience that she began to lead the financial ministry at Ginghamsburg four years ago. But her financial transformation was not complete.

Shannon's next *Christian Wallet* conversion was to become a "conscious spender." A few years ago she started serving at Isaiah's Threads in the urban community of Trotwood, Ohio. Isaiah's Threads is one of Ginghamsburg's three gently used retail stores that support community outreach and is located next to our Trotwood-based campus called The Point. Isaiah's also carries fair-trade items. Shannon's exposure to fair trade at Isaiah's Threads combined with her mission-trip experiences to Ghana, Colombia, and Haiti opened her eyes as to the possibility of what fair-trade products could accomplish in the world. She began to value purchasing a product that was benefiting people living in economically difficult places where opportunity was limited and employment abuses flourished, like those she had met in her travels. "I love it when I buy a fair-trade product that has the producer's personal story attached. I feel like I am in partnership with the hard-working farmer who grew the crop or the woman who wove the fabric of my new shirt." Shannon became increasingly concerned about ethical treatment for workers globally and determined to use her wallet to begin making a difference.

I asked Shannon how she managed to buy fair-trade products, which tend to be more expensive, within her budget and modest income. "I focus much more on quality than I do quantity. Most of us have overflowing closets. We need to shift our focus. I can buy more clothes regardless of who produced them and have more options, or I can settle for fewer items but wear them with a clean conscience. I can choose more, or I can choose fair. I want to better the world through my purchases."

Shannon is also an advocate of shopping for used clothing. She pointed out that regardless of where the product was originally made, by buying it secondhand she is living "greener" while also keeping the dollars spent out of the hands of the abusers of labor. "Visit your local gently used store and dig through the racks. You will keep your dollars in your own community and serve your neighbors," Shannon shared. Over the past year, she committed to wearing either one fair-trade item or one used item each day as part of her wardrobe.

Shannon advised those who want to become conscious spenders to start by educating themselves via fair-trade websites and blogs. She indicated that fair-trade coffees, teas, and chocolates are the easiest to find in most communities and to initiate new buying habits with those. Shannon quoted author L. N. Smith: "Every dollar you spend . . . or don't spend . . . is a vote you cast for the world you want."[24]

PART II

How We Give

4

Generosity

One of my favorite contemporary theologians is Bono of U2 fame. Bono is unapologetic about his commitment to Jesus Christ wherever he goes. Bill Hybels, the senior pastor of Willow Creek Community Church in Chicago, Illinois, sat down with Bono a few years ago for a conversation about faith. Bono pointed out during their dialogue that 2,003 Scripture passages pertain to the poor, the largest quantity next to those Scriptures dealing with personal redemption and salvation. Bono proclaimed that "the main thrust of the Scriptures is to meet Christ through working with the poor and disadvantaged." He referenced Matthew 25, the only part of the Gospels in which Jesus described judgment day. I have always referred to that as the "final exam" passage. To pass that final, we had better belong on the side of those who clothed the naked, fed the hungry, and visited the prisoner.

Bono next asked a great question: "Why have we amassed all this wealth and power if we cannot go to the aid of our sisters and brothers?. . . Love thy neighbor is not advice; it's a command." He followed up with two more excellent questions:

"Can an accident of longitude and latitude really decide whether you live or whether you die? In the global community—in the globalized world, can you say . . . because that's happening over there, it's not really my concern? Well, you can't if you're a Christian."[1]

I was born to a middle-class family in Cincinnati, Ohio. When compared to the majority of people in the world it means that I was also born into great privilege. I am thankful for that. But, does that mean that God favors me personally more than he does a mother in Darfur, Sudan, who is working hard to raise her children alone after her husband was murdered? Am I more favored because of my more privileged "accident of longitude and latitude"? "Privilege" should not imply a favored status but a responsibility.

As people of privilege, our responsibility to the poor, widowed, and orphaned is made plain throughout God's Word. This book cannot cover all two thousand passages, but let's look at a key example in the Old Testament before we move to what Jesus reinforced in the New Testament.

The word *deuteronomy*, the name of the fifth book in the Old Testament, means "second law." In Deuteronomy Moses reminded the people before he died of the miracles God had performed and the provision God had provided on their behalf as they escaped Egypt and traveled the desert for forty years. Moses also reiterated to them what would be expected of them as God's "chosen" and privileged people. Chapters 12 to 26 comprise the Deuteronomic Code and provide a series of commands to the Israelites about how they were to conduct themselves when they reached the promised land. "These are the decrees and laws you must be careful to follow in the land that the LORD, the God of your fathers, has given you to possess— as long as you live in the land" (Deut. 12:1). In other words, Moses was saying, "This is the stuff you had better get right."

In speaking of the tithe in chapter 14 (*tithe* is defined as the first tenth of all of your income), Moses reminded the people of their responsibility to "the aliens, the fatherless and the widows who live in your towns." It was the people's responsibility to ensure that the disenfranchised could "come and eat and be satisfied" so that "the LORD your God may bless you in all the work of your hands" (Deut. 14:29).

Chapter 24 then particularly hones in on what God required:

- "Do not take advantage of a hired worker who is poor and needy." (v. 14)
- "Do not deprive the alien or the fatherless of justice, or take the cloak of a widow as a pledge." (v. 17)
- "When you are harvesting in your field and you overlook a sheaf, do not go back to get it. Leave it for the foreigner, the fatherless, and the widow." (v. 19)
- "When you beat the olives from your trees, do not go over the branches a second time. Leave what remains for the foreigner, the fatherless, and the widow." (v. 20)
- "When you harvest the grapes in your vineyard, do not go over the vines again. Leave what remains for the foreigner, the fatherless, and the widow." (v. 21)

Clearly, we are not to consume everything we produce. We were not created to be the consumers of stuff; we are to be the producer of God's provision and blessings into the lives of others—especially those who struggle to provide for themselves. Some form of the word "widow" appears in Scripture more than eighty times; "orphans" and "the fatherless" are referenced at least fifty times.

In Luke 4 Jesus declares his mission statement to the world, quoting Isaiah 61:1: "The Spirit of the Sovereign LORD is on me, because the LORD has anointed me to preach good news to the poor." If the gospel as we demonstrate it in the world does not serve the poor, then it is not the good news! Our privilege, our fortunate accident of longitude and latitude, carries deep responsibility.

In Jesus' brief three-year ministry on planet earth, he repeatedly modeled compassion for the least and the lost—not to mention for the downright sick or hungry. Yes, he came to share the good news, but his compassion also led him to practical action. When Peter's mother-in-law was ill, he healed her. If a demon needed to be cast out, he cast it out. If people were hungry, he fed them.

We see two specific examples of Jesus feeding hungry people in Matthew 14 and 15. Let's look at the first account starting in Matthew 14:13. Jesus had just learned that his cousin John (the "Baptist") had been executed by Herod. Jesus had suffered an egregious spiritual and emotional loss, so he climbed into a boat to grieve in a solitary place. Yet the crowds followed him. Any of us could have understood Jesus turning people away at that point, but he did not. "When Jesus landed and saw a large crowd, he had compassion on them and healed their sick" (v. 14).

As the day wore on, turning into evening, Jesus' disciples urged him to send the crowds away to the villages so that they could buy food. Isn't that so like us? Let me send these hungry people away or turn away myself so that I avoid responsibility. Jesus did not make it that easy. He demurred, insisting, "'They do not need to go away. You give them something to eat'" (v. 16). You are probably familiar with the rest of this well-known story. The disciples found five loaves of bread and two fish, Jesus gave thanks for God's provision, and five thousand households were fed. Note that Jesus turned the fishes and loaves over to the disciples as his distribution system; he didn't pass it out himself. We will visit this again in chapter 5.

In Matthew 15, we again see Jesus' compassion. At the end of another long day of healing, Jesus called the disciples to his side and said, "'I have compassion for these people; they have already been with me three days and have nothing to eat. I do not want to send them away hungry, or they may collapse along the way'" (v. 32). This time, Jesus relied on God's provision of seven loaves of bread and a few fish to feed four thousand households. What did Jesus not do? He did not claim that the hungry people were not his problem and avert his eyes.

Jesus' compassion drove him to heal and feed the throngs of people around him. Jesus also said to his disciples, " 'Whoever believes in me will do the works I have been doing, and they will do even greater things than these'" (John 14:12).

The word *compassion* is a familiar one, but it intrigued me the last time I read through these passages, so I looked it up. It literally means "to suffer together," to embrace the suffering of others. We claim to be Christ followers yet find it incredibly easy to ignore others' suffering. In essence we are saying, "It's not really my concern." But as Bono chastised us, "You can't [say that] if you're a Christian." God requires us and our Christian wallets to share in the suffering of and give proactively on behalf of all of our sisters and brothers.

TITHES AND OFFERINGS

We noted in chapter 2 that according to the Bureau of Labor Statistics (BLS), on average each American consumer unit gives $1,834 (or 3.6 percent) of its annual income to charitable or religious organizations.[2] Of that total, $699 goes toward "religious" giving. With each household on average making $63,784 a year before taxes, giving to churches is far below the tithe (10 percent) that Moses laid out for the people in Deuteronomy.[3]

Each year, Giving USA Foundation and its research partner, the Indiana University Lilly Family School of Philanthropy, issues a report about the state of charitable giving in the United States. The most recently published report at the time of this writing covers 2013 numbers. According to the research, there is some good news and some bad news on how Americans give toward what they consider to be important causes or programs. In 2013, Americans gave $335.17 billion collectively to charity. The good news is that "2013 marked the fourth straight year of increased giving," reflecting a 22 percent increase since the official end of the recession in 2009, or 12.3 percent after adjustment for inflation. The news was not so optimistic on the church front. Giving USA reported that giving to religious organizations was flat (minus 0.2 percent) between 2012 and 2013, with an estimated $105.53 billion in contributions. Adjusting for inflation indicates that giving to churches and other religious organizations dropped 1.6 percent.[4]

Christians give 2.5 percent of their income per capita, and tithers make up only 10–25 percent of a normal congregation.[5] Collectively, we do not do any better in our per capita giving than a non-Christian. Why do Christians not tithe? I believe there are a number of reasons.

First, we like to argue about the validity of the tithe. Many claim that it was simply an Old Testament commandment because Jesus does not specifically mention it in the Gospels. I could write a separate book about why some believe the tithe is irrelevant under the New Covenant whereas others consider it just as crucial today as it has ever been. I fall on the latter side of this argument for both practical and scriptural reasons. First, the needs of the world and all of God's children to be served through the church have not diminished since Old Testament days; they have multiplied. We are the only bank account God has for accomplishing his mission on planet earth. I believe we not only need to tithe on our income but we need to give additional offerings out of our wealth to reach the lost, feed and clothe the poor, and set the oppressed free.

Scripturally, I do not find anything that would negate the law of the tithe. Many say the tithe is "old covenant" since Jesus didn't command it. I would argue, on the other hand, that Jesus not only expects the tithe but also requires a generosity and investment that exceeds it. In the Gospels of Luke and Matthew, we see Jesus chastising the Pharisees for following the legalistic mandate of the tithe without an accompanying generous spirit. "'Woe to you Pharisees, because you give God a tenth of your mint, rue and all other kinds of garden herbs, but you neglect justice and the love of God. You should have practiced the latter without leaving the former undone'" (Luke

11:42). Similarly, Matthew 23:23 states, "'Woe to you, teachers of the law and Pharisees, you hypocrites! You give a tenth of your spices—mint, dill and cumin. But you have neglected the more important matters of the law—justice, mercy and faithfulness. You should have practiced the latter, without neglecting the former.'" Jesus made it a both/and choice, not an either/or.

Another reason that I am a firm believer in the tithe is that I have seen the fruits of faithful tithing and biblical financial practices within my own life. God "has opened the floodgates" and blessed us richly. Carolyn and I have been equipped to live well fed, sheltered, and clothed and to bless others in return. *Christianity Today* reported on the results of another five-year study released by State of the Plate. The study's report indicated the following: "Tithers carry much less debt than most people and are financially better off than Christian non-tithers—80% of 'tithers' have no unpaid credit card bills; 74% have no car payments; 48% own their home; and 28% are completely debt-free."[6]

Contention exists even within the ranks of those who believe in tithing. Does God expect us to tithe on gross income or net (after tax) income? Frankly, I prefer God's "gross" blessings for obedience to the tithe versus "net" or leftover blessings.

Perhaps the most well-known Scripture on tithing is Malachi 3:10: "'Bring the whole tithe into the storehouse, that there may be food in my house. Test me in this,' says the LORD Almighty, 'and see if I will not throw open the floodgates of heaven and pour out so much blessing that there will not be room enough to store it.'"

The State of the Plate report also provided insight as to other reasons Christians say they do not tithe: "38% say they can't afford it; 33% say they have too much debt; and 18% said their spouse does not agree about tithing."[7] Underlying most, if not all, of these reasons is fear or a lack of trust. Many times we choose to view our resources only through the eyes of earthly economics versus kingdom of God economics.

GIVING IN TRUST

I remember preparing for Ginghamsburg's annual stewardship series in the fall of 2008. Those were frightening days within the U.S. and global economy. The housing bubble had burst with a bang; significant financial institutions like Lehman Brothers, Merrill Lynch, Citigroup, and AIG either failed, were acquired, or were subject to government takeover. The stock market declined rapidly, and many, like me, watched chunks of their retirement savings being wiped out. Homeowners found themselves upside down in their mortgages, and many would go on to lose their homes. To add pain to disaster locally, GM, historically one of the largest employers in the Dayton, Ohio, area (the midsize city just south of Ginghamsburg), had announced plans to close its final Dayton plant in December. These were tough days for me, our attendees, and even the world. The biggest economic downturn since the Great Depression was entering full swing. Clearly this was not the ideal time to approach the congregation about God's call to honor him with the firstfruits of their finances.

As I was preparing for the series, God brought to my attention a lesser-known story from chapter 32 of the book of Jeremiah. That story, as well as the rest of that stewardship series, served as the foundation for my book *Upside Living in a Downside Economy*.[8] It is 588 BC when the story takes place, and the city of Jerusalem was basically under siege by the Babylonians. Jeremiah, God's chosen prophet and voice, was being held under arrest by his own king, King Zedekiah. Apparently Jeremiah and I share a spiritual gift—the gift of irritation. Jeremiah was labeled a traitor because he had been prophesying against his own people, holding them accountable for the dire straits in which they found themselves. The Israelites had turned their backs on the living God and were serving idols made with human hands. Sound familiar? How many of us too have placed more faith in the idols of our own making, our stuff and the debt that accompanies it, than we do in God? We worship the created instead of the Creator. We may not admit it, but our calendars and bank statements attest to it.

God had revealed to Jeremiah that Jerusalem was going to fall and that the people of Israel would remain in captivity for a long period of time. Jeremiah himself would never come back from Babylon, where the captives were exiled. Yet in Jeremiah 32:6–7, God asked Jeremiah to do the strangest thing—and stranger yet, Jeremiah went on to do it.

God directed Jeremiah to use his money to buy a piece of property that was very soon to be worthless as it fell into the invaders' possession. Jeremiah was to use what was in his hand, his finances, as seed money for God's future harvest—God's promise that the people would one day return to their homeland.

After Jeremiah had made the purchase and had the paperwork witnessed, he handed the deed of purchase over to a man named Baruch:

"'This is what the LORD Almighty, the God of Israel, says: Take these documents, both the sealed and unsealed copies of the deed of purchase, and put them in a clay jar so that they will last a long time. For this is what the LORD Almighty, the God of Israel says: Houses, fields and vineyards will again be bought in this land.'"

(Jer. 32:14–15).

Jeremiah then prayed, and God answered: " 'I am the LORD, the God of all humankind. Is anything too hard for me?'" (Jer. 32:26). When we fail to open up our hands, when we refuse to trust God with our finances, we are in essence responding to God's question, "Yes, Lord, apparently there are things we think it is too hard for you to do."

God cannot increase what we refuse to release. Jesus explained it like this: "'Very truly I tell you, unless a kernel of wheat falls to the ground and dies, it remains only a single seed. But if it dies, it produces many seeds'" (John 12:24).

The Bible is filled with seemingly irrational people like Jeremiah who were obedient to God when it made absolutely no sense by earthly measures:

- Noah, in the midst of what was essentially an arid desert, built a boat to save God's creation from an impending flood. (Gen. 6–7)
- Abraham (when still Abram) left his comfortable and financially secure home at the age of seventy-five to travel, at God's request, to lands completely unknown to him. (Gen. 12)
- Queen Esther risked her life by coming before the king of Persia unbidden to plead for her people. (Esth. 4–5)
- The prophet Hosea married a prostitute at God's directive. (Hos. 1)

We either believe that "God will meet all [our] needs according to his glorious riches in Christ Jesus" (Phil. 4:19), or we don't. We must "fix our eyes not on what is seen, but on what is unseen. For what is seen is temporary, but what is unseen is eternal" (2 Cor. 4:18).

Not only does God meet our needs when we release what is in our hands, but we also become God's economic delivery system for serving the least and the lost. As the living, breathing body of Christ, we are the only hands, feet, and wallet God has to accomplish God's work within the world. Have you ever heard a preacher insist, "God doesn't need your money. God can do it without your money. You just need to give!" That's true, we do need to give; but frankly, I find the rest of that claim misleading at best and bogus at worst. We are the only bank account that God has. God needs our feet, our hands, our money, and our trust.

I am in my sixties; as I regularly remind my congregation based on the scope and space of a normal lifetime, I am almost dead. James reminds us, "What is your life? You are a mist that appears for a little while and then vanishes" (Jas. 4:14). Jesus indicated that when we tightly grip the seed we have been given, using it only for ourselves, ultimately it will rot. But if we are willing to give it up, to entrust it into God's soil, then the seed grows into God's future harvest.

My daughter and son-in-law used to live in Boston, and during one of our visits Carolyn and I took a detour to visit the Breakers in Newport, Rhode Island, a mansion built by Cornelius Vanderbilt II in the mid-1890s as a "summer home" for when his estate in North Carolina, the Biltmore, got too hot and humid. This summer "cottage" was expansive and beautiful, encompassing 62,482 square feet of living area across five floors. One of the most impressive rooms was the library, filled with leather-bound books that no one ever reads on shelves made from beautiful wood. The tour guide indicated that the library had been built in Europe, disassembled, and then shipped to the United States for reassembling. The gardens also were impressive. The place is now a museum, a tourist attraction. Ironically, the tour guide revealed, Cornelius only visited his new vacation home four times before dying of a cerebral hemorrhage in 1899 at the age of fifty-five.

You can't take it with you.

GENEROSITY AS WITNESS

As we have discovered, our giving is God's economic engine for serving the world. And as we resource the world, God resources us. One of my favorite passages of Scripture is found in Matthew 6: " 'Do not worry, saying, "What shall we eat?" or "What shall we drink?" or "What shall we wear?"' For the pagans run after all these things, and your heavenly Father knows that you need them. But seek first his kingdom and his righteousness, and all these things will be given to you as well'" (vv. 31–33).

Our generosity, however, is critical above and beyond serving God's mission in the world. It is also essential to how we evangelize. We have to *be* the gospel before others will *see* the gospel. First John 3:16 says, "This is how we know what love is: Jesus Christ laid down his life for us. And we ought to lay down our lives for our brothers and sisters." The world will experience the love of Jesus when they see it in us, when they see it in action. James gets straight to the point: "As the body without the spirit is dead, so faith without deeds is dead" (Jas. 2:26). Sadly, "love" is often not the world's first experience of us when they see how we deploy our Christian wallets, not just in charitable giving but in everyday life. Tipping is a great example.

I recently googled the words "Christians" and "tipping" together and received 397,000 hits in .26 seconds. I confess that I didn't scroll through all of them, but I would have to guess that next to none of the 397,000 were flattering. The first returned headline was from *Christianity Today*: "Why Are Christians Such Bad Tippers?"[9] Secular media also chimed in, with two first-page hits from Huffingtonpost.com. If you are familiar with political satirist and comedian Bill Maher, you are no doubt aware that he is not exactly a fan of Christianity, or any other religion for that matter. On that first page of returned Google hits, I found an article from Dailykos.com that provided a transcript from one of Maher's shows, and the focus was Christian tipping. To give a few excerpts:

- "I keep seeing stories in the news about Christians stiffing servers in restaurants. Like the Applebee's waitress in Missouri who got this note from a church pastor. Written on the check, it said, 'I give God 10 percent. Why do you get 18?' Prompting the question, who ordered the piping hot a__hole?"
- *(Displaying a picture of a fake $10 bill)* "It's a phony $10 bill that Christians sometimes leave on the table in lieu of an actual tip. It looks like a $10, so you get the benefit of giving poor people hope, and then crushing it, but on the back it says, 'Some things are better than money . . . like your eternal salvation that was bought and paid for by Jesus going to the cross.' Yeah, well, Jesus didn't have to put gas in the donkey."
- "In Kansas, where instead of a tip a Christian family left their server, who they knew was gay, this note: 'Thank you for your service, it was excellent. That being said, we

cannot in good conscience tip you, for your homosexual lifestyle is an affront to God. Queers do not share in the wealth of God, and you will not share in ours.'"[10]

Ouch. That hurts. And the stories are probably all true. What is the use of our "Christian" wallets demonstrating to the world about Jesus? Even something as seemingly inconsequential as tipping can make or break our witness.

Our generosity, or lack thereof, also serves as a witness to our children and grandchildren. Many of us intentionally work to train our kids about giving and generosity, and this is a good thing, but we know that children grow up to demonstrate more of what they "caught" from us versus what they were actually "taught." I remember receiving my allowance as a child and being required by my parents to give my 10 percent back to God on Sunday morning. Recently Carolyn and I were traveling through the mountains of North Carolina on a weekend and stopped at a small, rural church for worship. The church had a small, white church bank on the stage. While the offering plate was passed for adults, the children came forward to place their offerings in the bank. This kind of formal lesson in giving is all good. But when we cheerfully place our own offering in the plate when it's passed in front of our children's faces and generously leave money on the table for our server at lunch, that's the message they will really take home.

This past fall Carolyn and I kept two of our granddaughters for the weekend. It was a great reminder for me as to how much fun, and how exhausting, spending time with the grandchildren can be. That weekend, Ellie, our then five-year-old granddaughter, was looking around the house and started noticing the framed pictures of Sudanese children. Since 2005, Ginghamsburg Church has invested over $7 million dollars into sustainable humanitarian projects for the people of Darfur, Sudan, and Aweil, South Sudan. Each Advent season, I remind our church family that "Christmas is not your birthday" and ask that they simplify their own Christmases by spending half of what they typically would and bringing an equal amount for what God wants to do in Sudan as part of a Miracle Offering. In 2009, I took my son, Jonathan, Ellie's uncle, into the war zone of Darfur to visit our projects, and Jonathan had taken many of the photos that had captured Ellie's attention. Ellie became very concerned about what was happening to these children in the Sudan, and I tried to share what I could at a level a five-year-old could comprehend.

Later, Ellie was digging through our collection of DVDs, intending to watch *Cinderella*, but her attention was commanded by a DVD about Darfur that Don Cheadle had sent to me. "Papa, let's watch this!" she said. I put it in but had to shut it off a few minutes later because it was far too graphic. Ellie became consumed with thoughts of the Sudanese children, so Nana Carolyn approached her with an idea.

Each December, Ginghamsburg Children's Ministry organizes a Sudan Bazaar to raise money for our projects. Families excitedly create kid-crafted treats and gift items to sell in their booths. In recent years, each bazaar has raised up to $20,000. Together, Ellie and Carolyn conspired to bake one of Carolyn's specialties, homemade cinnamon rolls, as Ellie's bazaar contribution. In the week leading up to the bazaar, flour started flying and the baking commenced. I smelled cinnamon wherever I went. The rolls were a hit and a sellout, and Carolyn and Ellie even took orders for later delivery. (I do have to confess that I gave their booth a little extra marketing from the pulpit that Sunday.)

Ellie did not have a bank account, but she used her passion to make a difference, with some help from grandma, by generously giving toward investing in kids' lives. It turns out that cinnamon rolls can be the gospel in action.

Carolyn and I deliberately focused on teaching our daughter, Kristen, and son, Jonathan, to be givers. We were almost too successful. For years after they left home, they wanted to continue giving toward ministry at Ginghamsburg even though they also had their own new church homes for tithing.

Carolyn and I were not the perfect parents, but we did intentionally work to ensure that we used our money in front of the children to demonstrate the priority of our values. Every spending decision is a spiritual decision because you are either positively influencing or negatively infecting your children with the values demonstrated by what you do with your money. It's not what we say or believe; it's what we do. It's how we are using our resources to demonstrate our commitment to the lordship of Jesus Christ.

I have never lacked for having a wish list. The Harley I have since sold was on that list for ten years before I could purchase it with cash. When the kids were younger, one of my wish-list items was a bass boat. At that point in my life, a favorite pastime was fishing, and I loved to take the kids. It was one of our bonding experiences. As we would stand on the bank with our lines and watch others glide by in their boats, I would sometimes say to my kids, "Someday Dad is going to get a bass boat."

A year or two later when our fishing experiences had become somewhat more infrequent, Jonathan and I were driving down the expressway and passed a man on the right pulling a nice bass boat. I distinctly remember Jonathan asking, "Dad, when are we going to get our bass boat?" I looked back at him and responded, "Jonathan, every year we give a bass boat and more to the church." He didn't ask again. Recreation, although important, should never exceed Christ's mission in our lives. Remember, every spending decision is a spiritual decision.

I wanted my children to know that when we live generously, trusting in God's provision and releasing all of our resources to God's purposes, we will change the world one life at a time. Mahatma Gandhi once said, "The world has enough for everyone's needs, but not everyone's greed."[11]

Generosity is for young and old alike; it is not generationally specific. However, as Ellie demonstrated, it does get lived out differently based on our age and life status. I want to issue a special challenge to people in my own age group. An article by Robert Love in *AARP The Magazine* recently pointed out that more than 100 million people are over the age of fifty. American adults in this age group are, all by ourselves, the third largest economy in the world, "trailing only the gross national product of the U.S. and China." Love also indicated that we together spend $7 billion a year just on online shopping alone.[12]

Robert Love focused on encouraging marketers to take notice, indicating that only "5 percent of advertising is directed at older consumers." I have the opposite wish. We have more disposable income—and more free time in most cases—than any other demographic. This is an incredible opportunity—and an even more significant responsibility. Rather than using this extra time and money on ourselves, let's use it to bless others—from the waitress struggling to make ends meet, to the student taking on more and more debt to pay for tuition and books, to the older adult without the money or transportation to make it to the grocery each week.

Jesus taught us that "'from everyone who has been given much, much will be demanded; and from the one who has been entrusted with much, much more will be asked'" (Luke 12:48). I suggest we start living like it; our final exam is approaching rapidly, and our "grade" may depend on it.

QUESTIONS FOR REFLECTION

- How much of your household income do you give away? Is there anything holding you back from giving?
- How can your generosity serve as a witness to the abundant love of God?

Meet Nate Gibson

Nate is in his early thirties and has served as the CFO at Ginghamsburg Church since his mid-twenties. He is also responsible for our business operations, leading the staff teams that serve inside our walls, including hospitality, bookstore/coffee shop, food service, and facilities. The annual church budget is close to $6 million and much higher if you add in the budgets of the three 501(c)3 nonprofits that Ginghamsburg launched and supports. Most twenty-somethings would have crumbled in the job within the first six months given that level of responsibility, but not Nate. He thrived, and he has executed brilliantly. Despite his heavy professional load, Nate and his wife, Krista, are incredibly strong young parents with three children, and Nate managed to earn his MBA and CPA also while serving full-time on our staff.

I attribute Nate's strength to three things: his deep faith, his atypical childhood, and Krista's and her parents' influence on a teenager who by all rights was better positioned to wind up in trouble than as a committed Jesus follower.

As a child, Nate lived with his mother and stepfather, his biological father absent from the scene. He was one of nine children, four of whom were stepsiblings plus one half-sibling. Nate's stepfather was in the U.S. Navy, so Nate's early childhood was spent in multiple cities along the East Coast. The family experienced continual financial struggles. Yet Nate as an adult shrugs that off. He laughed when we spoke and said, "I thought everyone was on food stamps and that Christmas presents were always delivered via the community fire truck or police cruiser. Who needed reindeer?"

When Nate's stepfather had two years left in the Navy, Nate's mom moved Nate and the rest of his siblings to Covington, Ohio, a small rural town thirty minutes northwest of Tipp City where Ginghamsburg is located. Nate was never sure exactly why she made the move.

Both of his parents struggled with substance abuse, alcohol being the drug of choice for his stepdad and alcohol plus drugs for his mom. Her addictions steadily worsened after the move to Covington, while at the same time she was struggling to support herself and the nine children. Nate's older sister started running the household, and at night after the children would be in bed, Nate's mom would go out. Nate's stepdad returned to the family at the end of his tenure in the Navy and realized how degraded his wife's condition had become. By the time Nate started high school, his four stepsiblings had moved in with their own mother. Ultimately his mother and stepfather's marriage ended in divorce.

These were difficult years. Nate's mom made more than one attempt on her life. Nate was the one responsible for saving her after one attempt, but he confesses that he contemplated not doing so. He had attended an area youth group a few times with a brother, which had been his only exposure to church, and he felt incredibly angry with God. "God needed to fix this." God did, over time, especially through the Meyer family.

Nate started dating Krista Meyer when they were both sophomores in high school. Nate described the Meyer family name as "the best you can get in Covington, Ohio." Krista's parents, Jim and Deb Meyer, and their extended family were pillars of the community, so to speak. Covington is a small close-knit community, so Krista's parents had to be well aware of Nate's family life, which was so different from their own. But, Nate said almost disbelievingly, "Jim and Deb never once cautioned Krista about me or even had a stern talk with her about our relationship. All I experienced in their midst was pure acceptance and love." Nate credits the Meyers, people of deep faith, and his older sister who chose to go on to college with giving him new images of what life could be like. Pursuing college became "natural after that."

After college, Nate and Krista married and immediately started great jobs right away as a young couple. "I think I made more money in one year than my parents had made in their lifetimes." At first, Nate admitted, "I just wanted to make up for what I had never had." That mind-set didn't last for long. His faith was deepening, Krista had a very compassionate heart for those in need, and Nate felt himself increasingly empathetic for those around him who were struggling. "I know what it's like to have nothing. I can put myself back there in a heartbeat. I had experienced living on food stamps." Nate also shared, "I felt a little guilty that God had chosen me to experience a better life. But, over time I realized that God had actually given me a tremendous responsibility. I *know* what it means to be without; I must do something about it."

Krista and Nate use their financial resources to serve the world around them. In addition to the tithe, they sponsor children with Compassion International. Twice they have purchased used cars for families in urgent need for transportation and have "loaned" funds for other car purchases, never expecting or receiving payback. Nate said, "Krista is an underdog champion and has a huge heart for the homeless. She buys a lot of grocery gift cards to give away and once delivered two bags of groceries to a homeless guy she spotted along the street." Both have traveled on mission; Nate has led six trips to New Orleans for Hurricane Katrina reconstruction, and Krista recently returned from Haiti. She has convinced Nate they need to invest in launching micro-business opportunities there.

I have also witnessed how Nate serves within our church family. At least twice that I know of Nate has recruited the life group he leads to roof two coworkers' houses. He uses his financial brilliance to assist those who can't afford professional service with their income tax returns, typically thirty to forty households a year. Nate shrugs it off, saying, "It's fun." He also recently helped one of our struggling small business owners get his books in order.

Nate, to me, is an inspiring example of what God can and will do when we turn our resources over to kingdom deployment. Nate's life could have turned out so differently. Only four of the nine children in his childhood family have not succumbed to substance abuse. He remains in close touch with his mom, ensuring that she remains part of his life. Nate concluded our conversation by saying, "As I have grown deeper in discipleship, I have learned how important it is to live life with an eternal perspective. I will be here for such a short time. I used to pray, 'God, help me and my generations make the world a little better.' Now I pray, 'Help me and my generations live and give with maximum impact.'"

5

Those to Whom We Give

As I prepared to teach our fall 2014 financial stewardship series, the Ebola crisis was in full swing. As demonstrated by the investment that Ginghamsburg has made in the Sudan and South Sudan for more than a decade, I have a heart for the people of Africa. Yet I had found it somewhat easy to pay little attention to this horrific infectious disease while I was safely ensconced in Tipp City, Ohio, on the other side of the Atlantic. The thousands of deaths remained a sad and troubling statistic, yet I had little heart connection.

One week, as I prepared my message, the news media reported that an infected nurse, who had provided care for the first person to die from Ebola in the United States, had traveled through Cleveland, Ohio. Two schools in Cleveland were closed; a thousand or more people were put under observation; and the nurse's fellow air travelers were screened. Suddenly the number was no longer simply a number. Ebola wasn't a twelve-hour flight away; it was potentially a three-hour drive away. This was a little too close to home!

In my message that weekend, as I reflected on how the proximity of the crisis took me so easily from near apathy to keen

interest, I asked a critical question: How do we expand our
hearts so that we have compassion for all of God's children,
whether near or far? The truth is, we are often blind to the crises
impacting not only the people God loves a continent away but
even those living on our own block. Few of us know the names
of all of our neighbors, much less the private traumas that may
be besetting their lives behind closed doors. Many middle-class
families, including those in our own neighborhoods, found
themselves trying to navigate church food pantries and sources
of public assistance for the very first time during the recent
Great Recession of 2009 and beyond. Did we know? Did we
care? The American middle class has been shrinking rapidly.
In 2014, the *New York Times* reported, "after-tax middle-class
incomes in Canada—substantially behind in 2000—now
appear to be higher than in the United States. The poor in
much of Europe earn more than poor Americans."[1]

Time magazine reported in July 2014 that 40 percent of
U.S. working-age families earn $40,000 a year or less. Most live
within 250 percent of the official poverty level, the eligibility
threshold for food stamps. The article goes on to give an especially sobering statistic based on current trends: "Half of today's
20-year-olds will receive food stamps during their adult lives."[2]
In total, 45 million Americans live below the poverty line.[3]

Those of us in the middle class who may be oblivious to the
emerging economic needs of our middle-class neighbors typically know even less about the lives of those who live in chronic
poverty and laboriously work through the lines, paperwork,
and transportation challenges to navigate public assistance systems every day to feed themselves and their children.

OUR RESPONSIBILITY TO OUR NEIGHBORS

We noted Jesus' compassion for the hungry in Matthew 14 in
the feeding of the five thousand. God's priority for the poor,
hungry, hurting, and lost must be ours. We cannot with integrity call ourselves Jesus followers and yet turn our backs. Notice

that Jesus did not conjure the food from thin air. His disciples collected the shared resources of the community; Jesus blessed it and multiplied it; and the disciples delivered it. We are part of God's economic delivery system. Never in Scripture will you read about money simply falling from the sky. God's means of provision is through God's people. That means us. We see the same principles at play in Mark 8 when we read about the feeding of the four thousand. When we trust and place our resources in the hands of God, *all* the people eat and are satisfied (Mark 8:8).

In Luke 12:35–48, Jesus tells the parable of a faithful and wise manager who is watchfully waiting and preparing for his master's return. Jesus says, "'Who then is the faithful and wise manager, whom the master puts in charge of his servants to give them their food allowance at the proper time? It will be good for that servant whom the master finds doing so when he returns. Truly I tell you, he will put him in charge of all his possessions'" (vv. 42–44). Jesus then goes on to describe what would happen if the manager abandoned his duty to give the servants their food allowances and instead used the master's resources for himself to "'eat and drink and get drunk'" (v. 45). Jesus concludes,

"The servant who knows the master's will and does not get ready or does not do what the master wants will be beaten with many blows. But the one who does not know and does things deserving punishment will be beaten with few blows. From everyone who has been given much, much will be demanded; and from the one who has been entrusted with much, much more will be asked."
                                                        (Luke 12:47–48)

Most of us reading this book are certain to be among those God would consider as having been "given much." I do not want Jesus to return only to find me abdicating my responsibility to the least and the lost.

God equips us with material and financial resources for the

meeting of God's purposes in the lives of others. Remember, Jesus didn't come to planet earth just to get us into heaven. That's one result, but it's not the mission-essential goal. Jesus' purpose is first to get heaven *into* us and then the resources of heaven into the world *through* us. We will be held accountable for the kingdom deployment of the resources with which we have been entrusted.

Matthew 25, appropriately the same chapter in which the "final exam" on judgment day is described, includes Jesus' well-known parable of the Talents, identified in some versions of the Bible as bags of gold. In the parable, a wealthy master (God) entrusted his financial resources to three servants during a long absence. The first two invested the bags of gold and were able to double the return in time for the master's home-coming. The third servant, however, buried his gold (perhaps "hoarded" would be a fitting paraphrase), explaining to the master that he was afraid, fearful the master would be upset should any investment go south. On the contrary, the master was furious. The gold should have been invested into the master's purposes, and the master should "'have received it back with interest'" (v. 26). The master directed the other servants to "'take the bag of gold from him and give it to the one who has ten bags. For whoever has will be given more, and they will have an abundance. Whoever does not have, even what they have will be taken from them. And throw that worthless servant outside, into the darkness, where there will be weeping and gnashing of teeth'" (vv. 28–30).

On the whole, Americans are fairly charitable people. As noted in chapter 5, *Giving USA 2014* reported that in 2013, Americans gave $335.17 billion collectively to charity, the fourth straight year marked by an increase in giving since the end of the recession.[4] Five types of charities in that same year reached or surpassed all-time-high-giving records since the end of the recession: education, human services, foundations, health, and environment. Giving to churches and religious organizations, however, declined slightly.[5]

Despite the uptick in overall giving, there were shifts in who was giving and to what extent. It turns out that the wealthy are giving less, and the poor and middle income are digging deeper. According to Charity Navigator, "The wealthiest Americans—those who earned $200,000 or more—reduced the share of their income they gave to charity by 4.6 percent from 2006 to 2012. Meanwhile, Americans who earned less than $100,000 (including poor and middle-class families with two working adults) donated 4.5 percent more of their income in 2012 than in 2006."[6] Who was it again in Luke 12:48 that said, "'From everyone who has been given much, much will be demanded; and from the one who has been entrusted with much, much more will be asked'"? Some of us had perhaps better hope that it wasn't Jesus.

For five years, the Charities Aid Foundation (CAF) has released an Annual World Giving Index. American readers will be pleased to hear that the United States was ranked as the world's most generous country. However, based on the criteria used to derive the ranking, many Americans may be surprised to hear that the United States shares that number one spot with Burma, a poor country that only recently emerged out from under a harsh dictatorship spanning several decades. How can Burma, also known as Republic of the Union of Myanmar, tie with the nation that has the highest gross domestic product (GDP) in the world? The rankings were based on three factors: helping a stranger, donating money, and volunteering time. Although the United States has a strong performance across all three categories, it only came in ninth in the percentage of its population who gave money, whereas 91 percent of the people of Myanmar donate money. This high percentage is attributed in part to the country's strong Theravada Buddhist community, in which an estimated 500,000 monks receive support from lay devotees. Charitable giving is considered integral to the practice of Theravada Buddhism. Sound familiar? Perhaps we American Christians should take note that we have room for improvement in our giving.[7]

LONG-TERM SOLUTIONS

Clearly, we are called to give generously—but not without discernment for giving where our money will truly help. I believe that Scripture calls us to do ministry with the poor through empowerment, not enabling—to give a hand up, not simply a hand out. Otherwise the poor and underresourced will never grasp a true lifeline to a better, self-sustainable way. In the last chapter, we read several verses from Deuteronomy 24 in which God directed the farmers not to glean to the edge of the fields but to "leave what remains for the foreigner, the widow, and the fatherless," so that the poor could then come in and glean for themselves. After Jesus fed the five thousand, twelve baskets of leftovers were collected so that the people had an ongoing way to sustain themselves. The future means of provision did not require another miracle.

By equipping folks with new strategies and giving them new tools, we promote dignity. People deserve dignity, and work provides dignity. Part of our esteem is found through our work, through what we are able to accomplish and contribute with our minds, hands, and gifts.

In typical church charity, we can sometimes do more harm than good. A newly unemployed dad depressed at Christmas time that he cannot buy gifts for his children does not need to have a logoed church van pull up with well-meaning gift buyers hopping out in view of his children to stuff the family tree with brightly wrapped presents and packages—and sometimes even bringing the tree itself! An empowering alternative would give the father a way to buy presents himself through the dignity of work. For the New Path ministry's Christmas family initiative, parents are given the opportunity to serve with New Path to acquire the "funds" they need to go in and "shop" for their own children at the New Path and Ginghamsburg Church–provided Christmas store each December.

This is why the outreach that Ginghamsburg provides extends well above and beyond material assistance, with GED preparation, job-skills training, and student-tutoring programs designed to help people break cycles of poverty and develop new visions for what is possible. Our local ministries focus on transforming lives and future generations. All of our humanitarian investments into the Sudan and South Sudan are designed with sustainability in mind. For instance, when we implement safe-water yards for arid communities, a small fee structure is established for those within the villages who can afford to pay. That money is all placed in reserve for future repairs and parts. Local members of the community are trained to be the ongoing water and sanitation committee that will ensure safe water is available for the generations yet to come.

GIVING TO AND THROUGH THE CHURCH

Let's return to the topic of the tithe that we first touched on in chapter 4. As I explained, I am firmly convinced in the power and purpose of the tithe, defined in Scripture as the first 10 percent of all that comes into our hands. The needs within the world are simply too great for those of us who call ourselves Jesus followers to turn a blind eye. I have also seen the fruits within my own life of what can happen when we faithfully invest that first 10 percent back into God's hands. I also noted that I can't find anything within Jesus' teachings that would set the tithe aside.

Even Christians who believe that the New Covenant did not set aside the tithe may struggle with what kinds of giving should be included in the tithe. Before the Ginghamsburg Church leadership board and senior staff leadership team interview prospective new board members, we check their giving and attendance records within our church database. We believe in the three-"W" approach to board member selection of wisdom, work, and wealth. Wisdom, or spiritual depth and discernment, is of course crucial. However, we also do not want people serving in board leadership who are not investing their work (front-line ministry) and wealth into what God is doing in ministry and mission via Ginghamsburg. Sometimes when we check the giving records of prospective board members, we are disappointed in what we find. Giving levels are not always commensurate with what could be reasonably expected based on what we know about their employer and/or role in the marketplace. Of course, we don't know folks' exact incomes, so we do call many of them for dialogue to learn more. When we ask about the tithe, it is not uncommon for someone to say, "But I do tithe! I may only give $X at church, but I support two World Vision children, frequently give to the American Red Cross, and help out my alma mater's athletic department." These are all good things, and I commend them. But they do not represent the tithe.

Perhaps the most famous verses on the tithe are Malachi 3:9–10a: "'You are under a curse—your whole nation—because you are robbing me. Bring the whole tithe into the storehouse, that there may be food in my house.'"

God's "storehouse" is the church. When the whole tithe, the full 10 percent, is brought to God's church, there will be plenty of food and other resources for those who need it. As individual givers we can do good in the world; collectively as givers, we can change the world. There is power in community as God accomplishes through the community of followers what we cannot accomplish on our own. The night Jesus prepared his disciples for his impending arrest and death in John 15:5, he said, "'I am the vine; you are the branches. If you remain in me and I in you, you will bear much fruit; apart from me you can do nothing.'" It is when we are connected not just to an organization of people but to the body of Christ itself—the church—that we can produce "much fruit." Without that intertwining of the many branches secured to the nurturing vine to produce the resources of heaven for planet earth, we are "'like a branch that is thrown away and withers; such branches are picked up, thrown into the fire and burned'" (John 15:6). Return to the story of the fishes and loaves. When the "community" listening to Jesus combined all of the resources that it had, the seemingly meager amount collected was exponentially multiplied into a miracle once placed in God's hands.

I love and appreciate what God has accomplished through the combined resources of the faithful givers and servants of the Ginghamsburg Church faith community. Our global impact in places like Sudan and South Sudan via the eleven years of the Christmas Miracle Offering has served tens of thousands of lives—so much more than any individual's offering can do alone. Locally, Ginghamsburg tithes, offerings, and servant hands and feet have made it possible to launch and support three 501(c)3 nonprofits over the past two decades: Clubhouse is an after-school, teen-led mentoring and tutoring program that serves at-risk children in six communities located near our three primary worshiping campuses. This year Clubhouse will hold 120 sessions for more than 450 children through the efforts of 400 trained teens and 85 adults. Our New Path ministries serve 57,000 people in our surrounding communities annually through both material assistance and life development programs. New Creation Counseling Center provides more than $325,000 of uncompensated, professional counseling care to neighbors annually, serving not only the insured but also the uninsured and underinsured.

It is only within our combined community and resources that God has the raw materials needed for miracles of multiplication and transformed lives. These are also empowering ministries and not simply enabling ministries. New Creation helps to restore mental, spiritual, and emotional health and hope to its clients. Clubhouse has a double impact—it equips teens to play significant leadership and coordination roles while helping the children served find academic success, spiritual hope, and enhanced pictures of what their futures may hold. There are very real material needs in this world, and New Path helps to meet those with food, furniture, clothing, cars, and medical supplies. However, a learn-earn-serve component is built into most of its ministry areas, helping clients attain and retain dignity. Before an applicant receives a car, for example, he or she must go through life-skills training classes, demonstrate enough income to fuel and maintain the car, and give back to others also in need by serving with New Path. New Path also provides GED programs and job-skills training, along with paid internships, to help individuals acquire the diploma, skills, and documented experience they need to find employment.

In community, Ginghamsburg Church, New Path, New Creation Counseling, and Clubhouse can accomplish far more than any one individual or entity could ever do. I love the story of Missy Marshall. Missy, who is part of our Fort McKinley campus in a significantly socioeconomically challenged part of northwest Dayton, completed the job-skills training offered by New Path as a first step on her dream of someday starting a catering business. New Path then employed her as an intern, providing experience and a small stipend, as Missy prepared lunches for YouthBuild participants. YouthBuild is an agency in partnership with New Path that employs low-income young people to work full-time for six to twenty-four months toward their GED while building affordable housing for homeless and low-income neighbors. Missy's next assignment was to be hired by Clubhouse to provide nutritious summer lunches for at-risk, hungry kids in three Clubhouse locations. In the meantime, New Creation partnered with Clubhouse to do group counseling as needed with Clubhouse kids.

Of course, Ginghamsburg Church is not the only faith community that has experienced God's exponential miracles of multiplication when the church releases its combined resources into God's hands. I recently heard the story of Life Church in Memphis, Tennessee, led by Pastor John Siebeling. Life Church is also located just a short drive away from what is known as the hungriest zip code in the United States, where 74 percent of the children go to bed hungry each night. On learning this, Pastor John and his wife felt inspired to invest $5,000 of their own money to purchase an old ice-cream delivery truck that could be used to deliver food to some of these children. Pastor John also cast the need and vision to the church family. That day, others brought forward $5,000 checks for a total of $75,000, allowing the church to purchase fifteen refrigerated trucks. Now, Life Church feeds 2,600 hungry kids each weekend at six different schools serving as distribution centers for weekend meals when schools are otherwise closed. Life Church is energized and growing as it feeds the hungry and offers prayer for kids who need food, a friendly face, and Jesus.[8] The congregation recognizes that it is God's economic delivery system to the least and lost.

When choosing to give your money to and through the church, you are expanding not just the mission but the message of Jesus Christ in the world. How are people going to know that Jesus saves, that Jesus heals, that Jesus provides, if the church that he founded, the church that bears his name, is not delivering?

CHURCH AND COMMUNITY PARTNERSHIPS

This type of community investment, however, should not be tightly gripped by only the church itself. Churches don't always have the resources or expertise needed to do certain types of work, and even when they do, sometimes there is no need to "reinvent the wheel," so to speak. Many community agencies are doing good work and are very in tune with the community's specific needs, but they may need more money and manpower to be more effective. Developing partnerships among and with other agencies, schools, governments, and local businesses (or other churches) can be powerful for transforming neighborhoods. Fort McKinley, as I mentioned, is a challenging place to do ministry. Its per capita income is estimated at less than $18,000 per year. More than 30 percent of its children live below poverty level. The houses in the neighborhood have often been neglected or abandoned. Drug houses and crime have exacerbated the neighborhood's challenges.

Ginghamsburg merged in 2008 with what was then Fort McKinley United Methodist Church, a dying church of about forty aging people who commuted in from various communities. Before the merger, in Montgomery County, where Fort

McKinley is located, a nonprofit affordable housing organization and a housing contractor had repeatedly applied for affordable housing grants from the state of Ohio to revitalize the blighted neighborhood and replace abandoned, crumbling houses with new homes. Three times the grant request was denied because the grant requesters lacked having a strong partner located within the community. However, once the Fort McKinley campus as a Ginghamsburg Church community started serving and partnering with neighbors and an active New Path office opened in the Fort's basement, the outlook changed. The Fort and New Path quickly started becoming the empowering center within the Fort McKinley community. The fourth time the requesters applied, with New Path named as the social services provider for the homes' future lease-to-own residents, the grant proposal was accepted, leading to the construction of twenty-five houses that are giving the neighborhood and the homes' occupants a new lease on life. This is the miracle of multiplication through the power of church and community partnerships in action.

GIVING BEYOND THE TITHE

When we are faithful in the tithe, God also gifts us to invest generously above and beyond the tithe. We are created in God's own image, and God is the original Giver. "For God so loved the world that he *gave* his one and only Son, that whoever believes in him shall not perish but have eternal life" (John 3:16, italics added). God's generosity has no limits. Although I firmly believe that the tithe must be our first place of financial commitment, I fully endorse opening our Christian wallets to other areas of our heart's passion.

Carolyn and I support several missionaries and ministries beyond the purview of Ginghamsburg Church. One of our primary commitments beyond the tithe is toward four scholarships we provide to students from my high school alma mater,

North College Hill in Cincinnati. North College Hill is a racially diverse school system in which 100 percent of the students receive free breakfasts and 90 percent participate in the free-lunch program. I graduated from NCHS with an incredibly poor academic record and would have faced limited future prospects if I had not met Jesus. A good education provides students with new life pictures and enhanced opportunities. For North College Hill students, a scholarship and the opportunity to go to college may finally break the bonds of generational poverty within a family.

The students who receive these scholarships have to work for them; they are not a simple handout. Recipients must have a 3.25 or higher GPA and be involved in service projects that enhance their school or community. The tithe is first in my heart, but this scholarship program for at-risk students runs a close second.

Whom has God placed in your path with needs for which you might be the source of a solution? What grabs your heart when you read the morning newspaper or RSS feed? What is happening with your neighbors, your school system, or your employees that may need attention? Do you need to engage financially and politically on behalf of a justice issue that you find compelling?

These are great questions to answer, but I don't want to ask them without including a disclaimer. Both as churches and as individuals we are most effective when we decide on a few key areas of focus versus using a scattershot approach. Every other minute it seems we are bombarded for requests for funds: mailed brochures, e-mail appeals, and TV commercials with mournful soundtracks featuring pictures of sad kids or puppies. Yet our resources are limited. It can be tempting to give a little bit of money to a lot of different organizations (and those organizations will be quick to remind you that "every little bit helps!"), but imagine what can be done when you invest your heart along with your money. Committing your money to a cause you are passionate about will always have more impact because those dollars are accompanied by your prayers, your time and energy, and your long-term, consistent support.

Consistency over the long haul is tough, especially when new, urgent, or "sexier" opportunities arise. Because Ginghamsburg has remained focused on Sudan and South Sudan for more than a decade, God has been able to work miracles again and again. We continue to give and invest even though the feel-good part of the miracle offering subsided about three to four years in. In 2013 Ginghamsburg made the commitment to raise $1 million over five years for Imagine No Malaria efforts in South Sudan. Imagine No Malaria is part of an overall United Methodist Church initiative in conjunction with other key partners dedicated to eliminating death by malaria within our lifetimes. In the fall of 2014, when we were working hard to raise awareness and funds within the congregation to battle malaria, Ebola was making all of the headlines. It had taken by that point over seven thousand precious lives. Malaria was not making headlines. Yet malaria every year claims seventy-one times that number of lives—mostly children and pregnant women. In our fast-paced culture, we often become distracted from efforts that require investment for the long haul. There is no doubt that all urgent disasters and mass sufferings need to be addressed. However, when you or your church feels a calling to a new, urgent place of humanitarian investment, I would encourage you to make it both/and giving, not either/or. Otherwise, the greater long-term evils in this world may never be conquered.

As prudent stewards, it is essential that we give wisely, holding recipients accountable for doing their part with the funds or resources provided. To whom much is given, much is expected. When we do invest, we want to ensure there will be a kingdom return on that investment. Before you start giving above and beyond the tithe to an organization, I would encourage you to do your homework. Two nonprofit organizations offer online information for assessing some of the larger

charities and nonprofits: Charity Watch (www.charitywatch
.org) and Charity Navigator (www.charitynavigator.org).

The Charity Navigator site also provides some good tips
for assessing your giving investments. First, you will want to
ensure the fiscal health of the entity you are supporting as well
as look into how accountable it is to its funders and how trans-
parent it is about its transactions and partnerships. Of course,
results are critical. Is the organization achieving its stated goals
that you are funding? We are also reminded that we have to
be realistic. Our money cannot typically go only to programs;
all nonprofits have administrative needs and must cover basic
administrative costs. Yet we can investigate the percentage of
the budget that is spent on overhead versus results to determine
if the administrative costs appear reasonable. Once you have
given money, follow up. Do not ignore or forget about outcomes produced. Ensure a return on your investment of God's
resources to the best of your availability.[9]

This applies to churches as well. As I encourage you to be
faithful in tithing to your local faith community, I also believe
we need to hold our churches accountable regarding how and
where valuable dollars are spent and what results are achieved.

As I explored in my book *Change the World: Recovering the
Message and Mission of Jesus*,[10] all church budgets have to cover
three areas: mortar, mission, and ministry. Mortar represents
capital expenditures, upkeep, utilities, facilities staff, and debt
servicing. Facilities investment is necessary, but I have to confess that it is my least favorite way to spend money. Large
building campaigns tie the missional hands of future generations of believers as they struggle to pay off mortgages and
maintain the brick. I counsel churches to think long and hard
before committing to new building campaigns. Our mantra at
Ginghamsburg is to "minimize brick; maximize mission."

The ministry line item in your church budget covers discipleship expenses—the investment made into people or resources
deployed *inside* your church walls to grow up disciples of Jesus
Christ of all ages for the transformation of the world. The

mission section of your budget represents all ministries that benefit those *outside* the walls of your church. At Ginghamsburg it includes the apportionments we pay to our denomination for larger United Methodist global outreach, missionary support, material assistance, and life-development ministries within surrounding communities, and so forth. Each year as we assess our budget, we want to make sure that ministry and mission are not being sacrificed on the altar of mortar. In a typical budget year, our mortar expenses run about 22 percent of the total budget. Mission receives 34 percent, and ministry (discipleship) consumes approximately 44 percent. What do those percentages look like for your church? Are ministry and mission results visible and effective? These are great questions for your church to ask itself.

GIVING TO INDIVIDUALS

I want to address one last area of giving that I am frequently asked about when the topic of generosity comes up. How should we handle giving toward the homeless we may encounter along the street or strangers who approach us asking for money? Harder yet, how do we deal with family and friends who ask us for money? These are difficult questions when we are trying to balance empowering versus enabling and make responsible assessments without harsh judgment.

In our *Christian Wallet* survey, 78 percent of respondents said they rarely or never give to individuals on the street. Whether we give or don't give, such interactions are almost always awkward and leave us wondering what the truly Christian response is to such people in need.

I recently spoke with Marcia Florkey, the newly retired executive director of our New Path Outreach 501(c)3, about her views on the strangers who ask us for money. Marcia certainly possesses wisdom regarding this issue. Not only did she lead New Path for seven years, prior to that she was the executive secretary for Women and Children Programs International with the United Methodist Board of Global Ministries based in New York City. In this role, Marcia also partnered with United Methodist Women and traveled the world, frequently in Africa and Latin America, on behalf of justice issues for women and children.

Marcia is a firm believer in pursuing justice for all of God's children. As we spoke, she reminded me that the key is often found in Micah 6:8: "And what does the LORD require of you? To act justly and to love mercy and to walk humbly with your God." She referenced God's deep commitment to justice throughout Scripture, particularly in Psalms: "The LORD is known by his acts of justice" (Ps. 9:16); and "Righteousness and justice are the foundation of your throne; love and faithfulness go before you" (Ps. 89:14). She is the last person who would encourage us to turn a blind eye to the needy or the lost. At the same time, she knows that the problem with most charity is that it takes care of the immediate needs but fails to capitalize on the relationship building that will be required for authentic life transformation. As Marcia explained, "We must use the emergency need or crisis that presents itself to develop a partnership with the person in need. Otherwise, it will always be enabling, not empowering. It will be relief, not life development. The solution may save the day, but it won't save a life." As Micah 6:8 points out, we must balance mercy with justice.

When Marcia lived in New York City, approach by panhandlers was an everyday occurrence, just part of the fabric of big-city life. She indicated that she seldom gave handouts. If a talented musician were playing with an open instrument case, she might give if she had cash available. It was offering payment for a service rendered. Marcia explained that our conditioning as Christians teaches us to be compassionate, which is important. But too often that compassion changes to pity, and pity does not equal justice. Based on her experience Marcia argues that we must go deeper in empowering and relationship building in our charity rather than simply handing cash out. Otherwise we risk enabling chronically unhealthy behaviors instead of empowering new life choices.

Relationship building is also powerful because over time our relationship with the one we are serving becomes one of mutuality. We start to see each other as people; barriers of cultural and socioeconomic divide are torn down. Those with whom we are connecting begin to experience value and dignity. The interaction becomes much less about the material tangibles and much more about the intangibles of love and respect.

Marcia concluded our conversation by saying that giving funds alone is not the answer:

> If money could solve the difficulties of poverty in the U.S.—if money could do that, then the billions of dollars the government and churches have put into poverty programs since the mid-sixties should have eradicated poverty by now—but it hasn't. There is a poverty of the heart on both sides of those who have, and those who have not, that keeps us from developing the God-inspired relationships needed to bring economic and social justice to all.

When it comes to people with whom we already have relationships—friends and family who ask for money in times of need—in most cases the best response depends on the circumstances and the nature of the relationships. Almost half of our survey respondents (48 percent) said that if a family member or friend asked them for money, they would opt to pay for something specific the person needed. Thirty percent said they would give or loan as much as was needed. Only 6 percent said they would refuse altogether. When it comes to our children, Carolyn and I do not loan them money, but we have provided gifts of cash or other resources at times to assist with real and important needs—and sometimes simply to bless them. I know the character and values of my children, and I can give with confidence. That may not always be the case with other family and friends who make requests. When we are approached by those in our circle for money, these questions still remain: "By giving this money, will I be empowering, or will I be enabling? Will my gift foster independence or ongoing codependence? Am I helping, or am I ultimately hurting?"

Bottom line—wisdom and discernment are required—not just emotional instinct.

One thing I can say for sure—I do not co-sign loans, even for my kids. Proverbs 22:26–27 warns, "Do not be one who shakes hands in pledge or puts up security for debts; if you lack the means to pay, your very bed will be snatched from under you." If the situation merits it and my resources can afford it, I may give my child a car, but I will never co-sign for one.

In Matthew 10:16, Jesus cautioned his disciples to be "'as shrewd as snakes and as innocent as doves.'" We are to apply wisdom and discernment when using our financial resources to serve others, while never forgetting the generosity of the God we serve—a God who demonstrates repeatedly that we are more blessed when we give than when we receive.

I have experienced firsthand that generosity toward others begets even more generosity directed back at me. God's "return" to us on our generous investment is an inexplicable, excessive, and exponential reserve of joy that is difficult to describe to those who have yet to experience it.

In 2013 I was part of an Animate publishing project, and one of my fellow contributors was my friend Shane Claiborne, who shared a perfect story for wrapping this chapter up. During an extended mission experience in India, Shane and his fellow travelers would throw a party each week for the street kids, children typically ranging in age from eight to ten who daily begged on the streets simply to survive. A boy with whom Shane had developed a relationship shared one day that it was his birthday. As a special treat, Shane bought him an ice cream cone. Shane wrote that the boy "was so excited he stared at it, mesmerized." Then, Shane continued, the boy "yelled at all the other kids and told them to come over. He lined them up and gave them all a lick. His instinct was: This is so good, I can't keep it all for myself! In the end, that's what this whole idea of generosity is all about. Not guilt. It's about the joy of sharing."[11]

Friends, what Jesus has given us is simply too good to keep for ourselves. Let's share it.

QUESTIONS FOR REFLECTION

- Do you give primarily to and through your church? Why or why not?
- How do you feel about giving directly to individuals in need, whether they be family, friends, or strangers?

Meet Jim Taylor

Seventy-two-year-old Jim Taylor has been in the car business for most of his life, opening a Ford dealership just north of Tipp City in 1977. He loves it. Jim likes to say that his longtime partnership with Ford and selling cars was no random coincidence and not a result of any hard work on Jim's part. "God has uniquely gifted me for whatever reason with the ability to serve people by meeting their transportation needs. I am exactly where I am supposed to be." Jim goes on to add, "It's like the parable of the Talents. God has given me a lot, and it's my job to double it. When I read the Bible, I don't see car ministry listed as a spiritual gift. But what God has given me through the dealership is a unique resource for serving others.

Within the Ginghamsburg congregation, I am not aware of anyone more attuned to "God appointments" than Jim. His ears and Spirit are always open to any ministry opportunity that crosses his path, and it has led to many fruitful investments.

A recent example: Two years ago, a newspaper article caught Jim's eye about a local family, one of many, in dire need for transportation to and from work. Jim ruefully noted that he almost missed the story. He had thrown the newspaper away but went back to retrieve it when he realized he wanted to recheck something in the Sports section. As he was digging through the stack of paper, the name of the story's author caught his eye, an acquaintance of Jim's, so Jim took the time to read the article. As Jim described it, "Something just clicked." As a result, Jim, in partnership with a nonprofit in the community, funded "Rides to Work," a new ministry with an office now based out of our original Ginghamsburg Church building (circa 1860s). Rides to Work also transports people in recovery to and from Ginghamsburg's Next Step recovery worship on Saturday nights.

This is not by any means the first time Jim has invested his financial and "transportation" gifts to serve within the church and local community. I don't have enough pages left in the book to share all of the stories of those whom Jim has served through the years by providing low-to-no-cost cars and transportation. Jim employs men at the dealership from the local men's shelter, trying to have at least one man from the shelter on staff at all times. When I dubiously asked him about how well those guys worked out, he shrugged and said, "Many don't make it. There are failures. But it is well worth it for the few who do." His dealership is also a great supporter of area churches in addition to Ginghamsburg. Just last year, Jim assisted twenty-four churches with their transportation needs.

God's call on Jim's life for missional investment has extended well beyond the car business. While running the dealership in 1990, Jim started noticing how difficult it was for families to get credit approval, often because of significant, lingering medical debt. At the time, he was on the board of an organization called Partners in Hope (PIH). Jim and PIH, seeing the critical needs of people with health problems, established a free health-care clinic.

Jim persistently keeps his eyes open as to where God is working and then evaluates how he can join in God's plan. His dealership itself "tithes," setting aside 10 percent of what it makes for missional investment. Jim helped fund and start a Christian radio station in Phnom Penh, Cambodia; used his entrepreneurial and business gifts to train and fund more than seventy men and women starting twenty-four microbusinesses in Jamaica; traveled with me to the war zone of Darfur, Sudan, to inspect our sustainable humanitarian investment projects; and even traveled to Cuba as an American "capitalist" to share with Cubans about how to build a better financial future. The man does not stop! As I write this, he is working on new microbusiness investment opportunities in Nicaragua for impoverished former residents of the infamous Managua dump and evaluating a ministry opportunity in Senegal.

Before I ended a recent conversation with Jim, I asked him about the rest of his financial practices. Jim said, "I have always believed in staying out of debt, even before I heard you preach on it. When my wife and I moved into this area in 1977, we had three kids and bought a nice but modest three-bedroom home with one bath. Even though we experienced financial success through the dealership, we stayed in that house for ten years. We certainly lead a nice life but a simple life. We are blessed." He then added as an afterthought, "You know, we never took exotic vacations or anything." I had to suppress a smile at that: Cambodia, Cuba, Jamaica, Nicaragua, Sudan, and more. Jim was right—no exotic vacations, just exotic, impactful mission.

I asked Jim about future plans to retire, but he wasn't interested in that discussion. "Operating a successful dealership helps make a difference in my ministry, providing funds to invest in missions internationally as well as locally. It's not about the amount of money the dealership makes; it's about what I can do with it."

6

Responsible Investing

I am an ordained elder in the United Methodist Church, a denomination that traces its roots back to John Wesley, an Anglican clergy member and theologian whose life spans most of the eighteenth century. Wesley was one of nine children born to a financially struggling Anglican priest and knew what it was like to experience poverty. Once he even had the traumatic experience of watching his father marched off to debtors' prison. Even though he felt himself called to his father's profession, as a young man Wesley did not feel called to follow him into poverty. Instead of serving as a parish priest, Wesley instead starting teaching at Oxford College, earning a comfortable income.

While at Oxford, a chance encounter changed Wesley's perspective on money. Charles E. White, in his article "What Wesley Practiced and Preached about Money," writes that one cold day Wesley had just finished purchasing some art for his apartment when a chambermaid stopped by for some reason, clothed in nothing but a thin linen gown. Wesley was suddenly struck by the thought "that the Lord was not pleased with the way he had spent his money. He asked himself, Will thy

Master say, 'Well done, good and faithful steward'? Thou hast adorned thy walls with the money which might have screened this poor creature from the cold! O justice! O mercy! Are not these pictures the blood of this poor maid?"[1] White continues,

> Perhaps as a result of this incident, in 1731 Wesley began to limit his expenses so that he would have more money to give to the poor. He records that one year his income was 30 pounds and his living expenses 28 pounds, so he had 2 pounds to give away. The next year his income doubled, but he still managed to live on 28 pounds, so he had 32 pounds to give to the poor. In the third year, his income jumped to 90 pounds. Instead of letting his expenses rise with his income, he kept them to 28 pounds and gave away 62 pounds.[2]

Wesley delivered his most famous sermon on money on February 17, 1744. His teaching was based on three key principles: Earn all you can; save all you can; and give all you can. Wesley noted during the sermon that money matters, pointing out that Jesus himself repeatedly talked about the right use of money. In a sense, Wesley also chided Christians for not placing enough importance on it:

> An excellent branch of Christian wisdom is here inculcated by our Lord on all his followers, namely, the right use of money—a subject largely spoken of, after their manner, by men of the world; but not sufficiently considered by those whom God hath chosen out of the world. These, generally, do not consider, as the importance of the subject requires, the use of this excellent talent. Neither do they understand how to employ it to the greatest advantage; the introduction of which into the world is one admirable instance of the wise and gracious providence of God.[3]

I find these words to still ring true, more than 270 years later, especially when it comes to investing. How many of us are planting the seeds today that will be required for tomorrow's future harvest? Carolyn and I were fortunate that we received wise financial counsel regarding investment at an early age, beginning our retirement portfolio when I was just twenty-four years old. One of my seminary professors in particular stressed to "clergy in training" the importance of securing their own financial futures and the beauty of compounding interest. The required retirement age for United Methodist clergy is seventy-two. I am now in my mid-sixties, and Carolyn and I started investing the maximum of what we are allowed to invest into retirement accounts once we had our children's college years behind us.

INVESTING IN GOD'S WORK

Investment is not only important toward meeting your and your family's long-term needs but also for ongoing investment into God's priorities. In other words, it's not all about us. I love the story of Martha Berry. Martha grew up in Georgia, the daughter of a Civil War veteran. As an adult, Martha became deeply concerned about the lack of quality education for the children of poor Georgian landowners and tenant farmers. Martha had a God-sized dream to provide schools for these children but lacked the financial resources to make it happen. One of her fund-raising forays was to contact rising industrialist Henry Ford for financial support. Reportedly, Ford turned her away, pulling a dime out of his pocket, tossing it onto his desk, and saying, "That's all the money I have in my pocket; take it, and leave." Although Martha had to be discouraged, she pocketed the dime and took it back home for "investment."

The seeds and plants it purchased became a prolific garden, and she took the proceeds of that garden to reinvest. Martha also photographed the harvest, sending evidence back to Henry Ford of his investment's results while she seeded the next season's garden. Impressed, eventually Ford became one of her dream's primary financial supporters. Soon a Berry School for girls and another for boys were established, eventually becoming

Berry College—all because Martha invested a throwaway dime into the seeds that would become God's future harvest.[4]

Investing matters. First, we have to be concerned about our own ability to care for ourselves when paid employment is no longer feasible or desirable. Alarmists frequently warn aging Americans that Social Security will run out of money within two decades. *USA Today* partially debunked that warning in October 2014, indicating that the Social Security Trust Fund will run out of reserves by 2033 but that doesn't mean that social security payments will stop altogether: "The SSA [Social Security Administration] believes that it will be able to keep paying about 77 percent of all benefits after that date, using Social Security tax revenue to fund payments."[5] That is somewhat reassuring while also alerting me that I had better not rely on Social Security alone to fund my family's future. I had better be a creator of wealth and simply not a consumer of it. "Creators" make financial decisions with a focus on the future, keeping in mind that each financial decision we make today impacts the quality of our futures, our children's futures, and the future of all who depend on us. "Consumers," on the other hand, are always working to serve the past.

Some Christians argue that if we truly have faith that God will provide, there is minimal need for investment. As Jesus reminds us in Matthew 6:31–32, "'So do not worry, saying, "What shall we eat?" or "What shall we drink?" or "What shall we wear?" For the pagans run after all these things, and your heavenly Father knows that you need them.'" Yet Jesus is also the one who shared the parable we studied in chapter 5 about the master (God) who went away for a long journey, expecting his servants to have made a financial return on his investments by the time the master returned home. We are to trust God for the seed, but we are to be God's coworkers for the harvest.

Scripture offers many examples of why it is important to invest in future provision for ourselves, our families, and our communities, and to maximize our earnings. Perhaps the first

biblical depiction of the importance of setting aside or investing in reserves for the future is in the Old Testament story
of Joseph, the favorite son of Israel, who is sold into Egyptian slavery by his envious brothers. A man of integrity, Joseph
quickly became a valued servant to an Egyptian official named
Potiphar, who made Joseph the head of the household. However, when Joseph spurned the sexual advances of Potiphar's
wife, she accused him of assault, and Joseph was soon imprisoned for a number of years. Joseph was only released when his
ability to interpret dreams accurately came to the attention of
Pharaoh, who had experienced a troubling dream of his own.
We pick up the story of Pharaoh's dream in Genesis 41:1–4:
"Pharaoh had a dream: He was standing by the Nile, when out
of the river there came up seven cows, sleek and fat, and they
grazed among the reeds. After them, seven other cows, ugly
and gaunt, came up out of the Nile and stood beside those on
the riverbank. And the cows that were ugly and gaunt ate up
the seven sleek, fat cows. Then Pharaoh woke up."

This first dream was followed by a second, in which seven
heads of thin and scorched grain swallowed seven full heads
of grain. God gave Joseph the insight to interpret the dreams.
Egypt was about to experience seven years of plentiful harvests
to be followed by seven years of severe famine. Joseph wisely
proposed that Pharaoh collect and invest one-fifth of the harvests from the seven years of plenty so that the people could
be fed during the years of potential starvation. Joseph was put
in charge of the program, laying the groundwork for a God
plan that not only fed Joseph and everyone in Egypt but also
led to a reunion with Joseph's father and brothers who jour-
neyed to Egypt to prevent their own starvation. God provided,
but God provided through Joseph's leadership and investment
strategy.

The book of Proverbs also has a great deal to say about the
importance of hard work, disciplined financial practices, and
investment for the future. Perhaps my favorite passage on the
topic is Proverbs 6:6–11:

Go to the ant, you sluggard;
    consider its ways and be wise!
It has no commander,
    no overseer or ruler,
yet it stores its provisions in summer
    and gathers its food at harvest.

How long will you lie there, you sluggard?
    When will you get up from your sleep?
A little sleep, a little slumber,
    a little folding of the hands to rest—
and poverty will come on you like a thief
    and scarcity like an armed man.

These verses nudge me to ask myself some essential questions: Am I storing for the future, and what am I storing? How well am I gathering? Our American cultures idolizes leisure to an unhealthy point, and too much leisure leads to poverty: "A little sleep, a little slumber, a little folding of the hands to rest—and poverty will come on you like a thief and scarcity like an armed man" (Prov. 6:10–11).

If you are employed as you read this, then I encourage you to remember that these are the "power" years for maximizing your work and investments for yourself, your family, and God's purposes. "The wise store up choice food and olive oil, but fools gulp theirs down" (Prov. 21:20). Paul told his young protégé Timothy, "Anyone who does not provide for their relatives, and especially for their own household, has denied the faith and is worse than an unbeliever" (1 Tim. 5:8). Those are strong words.

WHAT'S HOLDING US BACK

Even though investing is important, many of us are not very good at it. The number of families in the United States who have IRAs and 401K plans has continued to decrease over the past decade. The 2013 Survey of Consumer Finances revealed a decline to 48.2 percent in 2013 from 52.8 percent in 2001.[6] A Bankrate.com survey in 2014 revealed that 26 percent of fifty-to-fifty-four-year-olds and 14 percent of those sixty-five and older have no savings. The survey also reports that "the median retirement account balance for all working-age households in the U.S. is $3,000, and $12,000 for near-retirement households, according to the National Institute on Retirement Security."[7] And most of those folks cannot be relying on pension plans. Sixty percent of Fortune 500 companies offered pension plans to new hires in 1998. By 2013, that had dropped to 24 percent.[8] According to the Bankrate.com survey, "Only 18 percent of U.S. workers say they are very confident of having enough money to live comfortably during their retirement years."[9] If so, then why is the 82 percent of U.S. workers who lack confidence not doing something about it?

At Ginghamsburg Church, I have preached for years on preparing for retirement via investing and about the remarkable results produced by compounding interest. Yet even many on our staff team have failed to act. As I write this, eighty-two of our staff members qualify for participation in the church 403b plan, the nonprofit equivalent of a 401k. Of those, 56 percent do not participate, even though the church as employer invests up to a 3 percent match on the first 6 percent invested by the employee. That is equivalent to leaving offered money lying on a table. Why?

I recently posed this question to Callie Brooks Picardo. Callie is married to Rosario Picardo, our executive pastor of new-church development, and previously worked as an investment banker. More recently, she has been a financial coach and served as director of giver services with a large Christian grant-making organization. Callie also comes from a long family line of financial advisors. Callie indicated from her experience that people typically are not investing in retirement options or investing in general for two key reasons: debt and lack of know-how. Callie does not believe that it is from a lack of "want to." As we previously discussed, both consumer debt and student loan debt are crippling many American households. In the case of our staff members, many are under the age of thirty-five, and student loan debt is a deeply challenging burden.

Also, many people feel uncertain about where to begin. In our *Christian Wallet* survey, 59 percent of respondents said they either don't have investments beyond a simple savings account (24 percent) or have investments but don't pay attention to them (35 percent). The Associated Press reported in July 2014 that U.S. students did not perform particularly well on an international test of financial knowledge and skills. Only 9.4 percent of fifteen-year-old students were able to answer the more difficult questions, and more than one in six U.S. students failed to reach the baseline level of proficiency in financial literacy.[10] The Chinese financial hub of Shanghai achieved the highest average score of the eighteen countries studied whereas U.S. students ranked tenth. Parents seem to leave financial training to the schools, and the schools largely seem to assume that parents are covering it. Only nineteen U.S. states require high schools to offer a course in personal finance. Ohio, the state where I live, is not one of them.[11] I challenge all of us who are parents to do a better job of equipping our kids, assuming we have first educated ourselves.

I asked Callie her best tips for getting started. Not surprisingly, she first counseled that people get out of debt before they even begin to invest. Investing for the future is crucial, but deciding to eliminate debt first is a simple matter of doing the math. From 1926 to 2013, the annualized return on stocks has been 10.1 percent; bonds are next at 5.2 percent, and U.S. Treasury Bills come in at 3.6 percent.[12] Those are very respectable numbers for an eighty-seven-year time span that also includes the Great Depression and a number of serious recessions. Yet today credit-card interest rates average between 13 to 15 percent, and many are higher, effectively wiping out whatever potential return on investment you might have received.[13] Callie did offer one caveat: if your employer offers matching contributions to a retirement account, if at all possible begin investing the amount required to earn the match. Don't throw that money away.

Callie and most financial advisors will next recommend that you build emergency savings before pursuing more intentional investing. Dave Ramsey, creator of the Financial Peace University curriculum, teaches at minimum you should set aside $1,000. He counsels that a fully funded emergency account is three to six months of your personal expenses set aside in a savings or money market account—funds to be used for unexpected life events like a job loss, unexpected baby, or home furnace replacement.[14]

When you are ready to invest, maximizing investment in your employer-provided 401k or 403b account is always a good start. Callie is also a fan of IRAs (individual retirement accounts), particularly the Roth IRA, in which you invest after-tax income but for which both earnings and withdrawals after age fifty-nine-and-a-half are tax-free. Traditional IRAs reduce your taxable income as you contribute, which helps lower your annual tax burden, but in most cases future distributions will be treated as ordinary income and may be subjected to income tax. For younger, smaller investors, Callie sees exchange traded funds or ETFs, as a potential option. ETFs are funds that typically track to indexes like the S&P 500, Dow Jones, or NASDAQ. So as far as investments go they are not too far off the beaten path. The best part is that some ETFs trade commission free, a strong plus for the more limited investor. However, you will need to do some homework.

Ultimately, your best investment is to find a money mentor or wise financial counselor, preferably one in line with your own Christian values, who can guide you through what can seem to be a bewildering morass of money-investment options. Proverbs 15:22 declares, "Plans fail for lack of counsel, but with many advisors they succeed." Proverbs 24:3–4 continues, "By wisdom a house is built, and through understanding it is established; through knowledge its rooms are filled with rare and beautiful treasures." A wise counselor can supplement your own wisdom, understanding, and knowledge to make the wise investment decisions. Of course, the use of our Christian wallets needs to ensure we are promulgating responsible investing and not simply unconscious investing that may finance companies and support endeavors that are the antithesis of kingdom-of-God values. We will return to that theme shortly. However, Callie noted that an organization called the Kingdom Advisors Group trains and certifies counselors from a Christian perspective—something to keep in mind if you seek professional counseling assistance. You can learn more at www.kingdomadvisors.org.

INVESTING WISELY

Wise investment is not a get-rich-quick scheme. It is a long-term, long-haul commitment toward God's preferred future picture. I shudder to think how many of us say we don't have enough money to invest yet drop $20 weekly on lottery tickets or take annual trips to Las Vegas, the epitome of the get-rich-quick mind-set. I remember watching an HBO-produced documentary called *Lucky*, which followed the life of some individuals who had won the lottery. One great line I still remember from *Lucky* was "Winning the lottery is like throwing Miracle Grow on your worst character traits." Most of the featured lottery winners would end up making very foolish and, over time, destructive decisions. One man purchased 1,200 pairs of pants, an airplane, and a host of other expensive items he didn't need, and probably ultimately didn't want. At the same time, I have to confess that I completely understand the appeal of this kind of thinking. As I watched the show, I remember fantasizing about what I would do or how I could spend $20 million dollars. In fact, I travel professionally quite a bit. How much easier would my life be if I owned my own jet? I could easily convince myself, "I need a jet. I need a jet for Jesus!" Then Proverbs 13:11 reminds me, "Dishonest money dwindles away, but whoever gathers money little by little makes it grow."

Sometimes as we age, especially if we have not done a good job preparing for our post-retirement futures, we are even more likely to make risky "investment" decisions. A couple in our church had practiced sound financial principles all throughout their lives and well into their forties. Yet as they approached their fifties, a friend shared with them a real-estate investment opportunity based on buying and rehabbing properties and quickly "flipping them." So the couple bought three houses, only to discover they lacked the skills to complete the rehab projects. By the time they paid professionals to do the rehabilitation for them, they took losses on the properties and almost lost their primary residence in the process. Be leery of risky investments. Remember, if you lose even 50 percent of your investment, you have to make 100 percent back simply to return to your financial starting point.

Others among us are too risk averse to invest wisely, only putting money into basic savings accounts. As I write this chapter, a 1-percent savings-account interest rate is considered top-notch for the market.[15] These folks need to remember that's why market investment is an "over time" commitment. We hear the stories, the constant reports, about market swings and instabilities. We can't panic. The stock market can be a great tool, and I encourage people to use it. But our security is not in the market—our security is in the promise of the One who is "able to bless you abundantly, so that in all things at all times, having all that you need, you will abound in every good work" (2 Cor. 9:8). I think the Greek words for "all times" in the New Testament means *all* times, including market downturns.

Note that the investment is not just for ourselves but so that we may "abound in every good work." Your investments are not just about meeting your personal future needs and desires and those of your family. They can also invest in that which will live beyond you. That is one reason why Carolyn and I created the scholarship program I mentioned in the previous chapter.

We know we can't take it with us, and we want our God-provided resources to create forward momentum for the generations that will succeed us. Think creatively about how your investments can serve your faith community or other causes that are important to you, regardless of your current investment level. Nate and Krista Gibson, whom you met in chapter 4, are a young couple. But they have taken out an additional life-insurance policy with an affordable monthly premium and named Ginghamsburg Church as the beneficiary. Of course, they first made sure their own children would be well provided for. If you sell stocks and make capital gains, you will be taxed on those gains. If you give those same stocks to the church for selling, the church will not incur the capital-gains tax. These are just two examples. A good financial advisor can help you develop a strategy for investing in God's kingdom purposes.

Although I have spent the first two-thirds of this chapter trying to convince you that investing is critical, I need to clarify that investing responsibly for the future is not the same as hoarding. Investing is not about getting all I can while I can simply so that someday I can retire to a leisurely life, a life of daily golf by the beach—although a little golf by the beach might be fine. As Callie noted when we spoke, "Retirement should not equate to living a life of complete leisure; it should be about eliminating your dependence on earning an income so that you have the freedom to serve the Lord in expanded ways." The Gospels of Matthew, Mark, and Luke all recount Jesus' saying, "For whoever wants to save their life will lose it, but whoever loses their life for me and for the gospel will save it" (Mark 8:35).

It is okay to have a bucket list of what you would like to do after you are no longer tied to earning a weekly paycheck. I would even encourage you to develop your dreams for a post-retirement future. Carolyn and I were just discussing our bucket lists the other day. One of hers is for us to take a picturesque train trip through the Canadian Rockies. One of mine is to spend a month living in Assisi studying Franciscan theology.

Carolyn and I made a brief pilgrimage to Assisi in the fall

of 2014, where Francis of Assisi in a wayside chapel received a mystical vision of Jesus Christ. An icon of the crucified Christ seemed to come to life before Francis's eyes, saying three times, "Francis, Francis, go and repair My house which, as you can see, is falling into ruins."[16] One of the churches we visited in Assisi was the Basilica of St. Clare, where Clare of Assisi, one of Francis's earliest followers, is entombed. St. Clare founded the Order of Poor Ladies, a monastic religious order for women in the Franciscan tradition, based on a theology of joyous poverty in imitation of Christ's life.

As I sat one afternoon contemplating a cross in the basilica, I reflected on the gospel's call to a sacrificial lifestyle as embodied in the life of Francis. I examined my own life and *Christian Wallet* practices in light of Matthew 6:19–20: "'Do not store up for yourselves treasures on earth, where moths and vermin destroy, and where thieves break in and steal. But store up for yourselves treasures in heaven, where moths and vermin do not destroy, and where thieves do not break in and steal.'" How well am I resisting the siren call of the daily marketing media blitz that feeds every consumer impulse imaginable? I have to ask myself, what exactly is it that I am investing in, and just as importantly—why?

In our investment practices we must constantly be cautious of the "bigger barn" syndrome. Look at the parable Jesus told in Luke 12 about a rich man who had experienced an abundant harvest: "'He thought to himself, "What shall I do? I have no place to store my crops." Then he said, "This is what I'll do. I will tear down my barns and build bigger ones, and there I will store my surplus grain. And I'll say to myself, 'You have plenty of grain laid up for many years. Take life easy; eat, drink and be merry'"'"(vv. 17–18). The parable concludes with the rich man dying that very night. Jesus warns his disciples, "'This is how it will be with whoever stores up things for themselves but is not rich toward God'" (v. 21). The rich man had failed to remember first the source of his blessing, and secondly the purpose of his blessing.

What I release to God's purposes is permanent and eternal;

what I keep for myself is temporary. I need to worry less about my stock market gains and losses today and focus more on my permanent kingdom net worth tomorrow and into eternity: "Remember this: Whoever sows sparingly will also reap sparingly, and whoever sows generously will also reap generously. Each of you should give what you have decided in your heart to give, not reluctantly or under compulsion, for God loves a cheerful giver. . . . As it is written: 'They have freely scattered their gifts to the poor; their righteousness endures forever'" (2 Cor. 9:6–7, 9). God increases our wealth when it's used for God's purposes. We can't serve God and money, but we can serve God with money. Be alert to the allure of greed. We are entering dangerous territory when growing our net worth and trusting our portfolio becomes our god instead of God.

SOCIALLY CONSCIOUS INVESTING

I believe that God not only expects us to invest but that he expects us to be conscious investors, carefully evaluating that in which we choose to deploy our dollars. As best we can, we want to ensure that we are socially responsible in our investments and supporting positive agendas. Investopedia describes two primary types of strategies for socially conscious investing: exclusionary and inclusionary. When you practice the exclusionary strategy, you try to ensure that you do *not* invest in companies that create products or propagate practices that you consider immoral or unethical. For instance, you may avoid companies that are somehow tied into alcohol, tobacco, pornography, weapons, or poor treatment of labor.

If you choose an exclusionary strategy, that doesn't mean you won't be tempted to change your mind now and again. I encountered a perfect example recently as I leafed through a copy of *USA Today*. The headline read, "Sin pays! Tobacco stocks light up." According to the story, tobacco stocks had risen 189 percent over the past decade. That's remarkable and grabs my attention as an investor. The reporter goes on to note, "Cigarettes might be an enemy of health officials, but the recent rise is a reminder of how they're an absolutely great business."[17] We have to consciously protect our Christian wallets from making decisions based on greed versus principle.

The inclusionary strategy means selecting companies or funds for your investments that support desired social goals. For instance, you may intentionally select a green technology company for investment, one that is working to create clean, alternative energy sources. Or you may select a stock for a company that is known for how well it treats its workers.

Either of these strategies is going to require you or your financial investment advisor to do some homework. In our survey, only 18 percent of respondents say they actively seek out socially responsible investments. If you're willing to do the research, there are a number of ways to find out more about the companies in which you may choose to invest. According to SEC regulations, a company with at least five hundred shareholders and more than $10 million in assets or any company that trades on an American exchange like the NASDAQ or New York Stock Exchange must make certain official documents accessible to the public. This is not the case for smaller companies, which therefore are more difficult to investigate. Some may still complete the filings, but it is by their own volition. Almost all companies have websites, and you may be able to glean information that way, or via their annual shareholder reports. Of course, discernment and a critical eye are required since companies have a vested interest in putting their best corporate foot forward in all of their communications. There are also research firms that specialize in providing reports to investors on company performance and other topics, but those are available for a fee.

Some funds also openly identify themselves as supporting certain values or causes. One example is Eventide Mutual Funds, which proclaims on its website that it "strives to provide its investors with the pride in knowing that their money is with not merely successful companies, but admirable companies."[18]

Given the time it takes to perform due diligence to ensure

socially responsible investing, Investopedia would recommend the inclusionary strategy over the exclusionary strategy for the private investor. Your personal refusal to buy a certain stock probably will not make a significant difference in the company's stock price. The impact of your attempted message may be muted. It can also lead to a slippery slope of asking where you draw the line on refusing to invest. For instance, do you refuse to invest in a technology company because at some point along the way that technology could perhaps be used in the delivery of pornography? You might be able to exert more impact by making investment decisions that are "for something" versus simply "against something." Regardless, we want to invest with intentionality, not blindly, from our Christian wallets.[19]

Divestment in a sense is also a form of an exclusionary strategy often applied to the investment portfolios of complete organizations. It occurs when an institution removes its financial support to promote a certain policy or behavior. Arguably the best-known historical example was the movement in the 1970s and continuing in the 1980s to sell off the stocks of companies that did business in South Africa during the apartheid era.

In a typical divestment scenario, activists raise awareness to create public pressure with the objective of lowering the targeted companies' stock prices and achieving concessions toward meeting activists' demands. One current example that frequently makes headlines is student efforts on various university campuses to force university endowment funds to divest from fossil fuel companies. Another high-visibility campaign in recent years focuses on divestment from Israel as a form of pressuring Israel to end its occupation of Palestinian territories. Many activists' efforts have focused on high-profile institutions like the Presbyterian and United Methodist denominations that manage large portfolios of retirement fund investments. As a United Methodist clergy, I should develop some awareness of how my future pension is being funded. I may find that I support the investment strategy, or my conscience may require that I become one of the activist voices calling for change. Do you know and support the investment choices of the organizations with which you are associated or from which you will benefit?

Ultimately, our most powerful tool for wise investment is prayer. Not "Lord, bless me to become rich" but "Lord, help me to be a wise steward; it's your money—not mine."

Before we wrap up the topic of responsible investing, let's touch briefly on another form of investment called microfinance. In microfinance, loans are provided to low-income or unemployed individuals or groups who would otherwise have no way possible to acquire funds for starting businesses. Ginghamsburg business owner Jim Taylor, whom you met in chapter 5, was one of the key people who invested in our microfinance ministry in Jamaica. As I wrote about in *Change the World: Recovering the Message and Mission of Jesus*,[20] I visited Jamaica in 2009 and was able to meet some of the entrepreneurs who had been mentored and funded by Jim and Jim's team. Jermaine, in particular, stands out in my memory.

At the time of my visit, Jermaine was a thirty-two-year-old fisherman with three children and a fourth child on the way. Jermaine had been left homeless at age thirteen when his grandfather died. While he was literally living on the beach, local fishermen befriended him and taught him their trade. Before he met our Ginghamsburg team, as a young father Jermaine struggled to support himself and his family with one well-worn wooden boat that he had owned since his teens. Like many parents, he wanted his children as adults to have far more opportunities than he had enjoyed. An initial microfinance investment into his business of $400, along with the development of a business plan with our team as advisors, helped Jermaine improve his boat and overhaul the small outboard motor so that he could not only fish but also ferry tourists to a reef used for snorkeling. Jermaine paid back the initial investment on time with 5 percent interest. He presented his second business plan for a $500 investment request during my visit. Jermaine's new plan was to purchase ten fish traps that would in essence do the fishing for him while he was ferrying tourists. Jermaine was on his way to reaching his dreams for his children.

Jermaine is not an isolated case. My research revealed that the default rate on microfinance loans is very low, typically estimated in the 2–9 percent range. Microfinance investment is also not limited simply to exotic or far-off locations. Our New Path Outreach 501(c)3 refurbishes mowers and provides small start-up investments to empower Fort McKinley community members to operate lawn-mowing services. These services not only serve Fort McKinley neighbors but also the surrounding township, which struggles with the upkeep of abandoned homes and lots.

I believe that microfinance is another opportunity for our responsible investment that makes God smile. Your small investments in the world of microfinance can result in big returns for those who live in difficult places. Some organizations, like Kiva, will position you to make microfinance loans for as little as $25. Learn more at www.kiva.org.

Responsible investing means taking all that God has placed into our hands and fully deploying it in every sense toward God's preferred future picture—both for our own lives and for the lives of others. Investing in tomorrow also requires a simultaneous trust in God's provision for both today and tomorrow. I was a teenager in the tumultuous years of the 1960s. The Vietnam War, racial violence, and campus unrest made for uneasy times. End-of-the-world predictions were not uncommon. Those bothered me. As a sixteen-year-old, I knew I was by no means ready to meet Jesus face to face.

My best friend in those days, Jeff, had a pool table in his basement, and pool was one of our favorite pastimes. Jeff's dad, Mr. Vorholt, was both an excellent pool player and a committed Catholic Christian. In his younger years he had studied for the priesthood before realizing that was not God's call on his life. Sometimes as teens we will listen to other adults while thinking our own parents are misguided and uninformed. Mr. Vorholt was one of those adults in my life.

I remember one Saturday night shooting pool with Mr.

Vorholt right after I had heard the latest "end times" rumor. I said to him, "Mr. Vorholt, this guy is saying that Jesus is coming again. If you knew that Jesus was going to come back in the next minute what would you do?" He glanced up from chalking his pool stick and simply said, "I would finish my shot." He must have glimpsed the bewildered expression on my face because he then turned to me and said, "Mike, I would finish my shot because everything I do, I do for Jesus, even if I am playing pool."

That is how I want to "responsibly invest" my life, living and giving my best in each moment toward God's perfect purpose.

QUESTIONS FOR REFLECTION

- How are you saving for the future? What are your long-term financial goals?
- Who is using the money you are investing? Does the way it is being used fit your beliefs and values? If the answer is "I don't know," how can you find out?

Meet Dave Zellner

I first encountered Dave Zellner at a conference that Ginghamsburg Church co-hosted in August 2014 with various United Methodist partners called "Walking with Palestinian Christians for Holy Justice and Peace." Dave, as the chief investment officer for Wespath Investment Management, which is the investments division for the United Methodist General Board for Pension and Health Benefits (GBPHB), was part of the GBPHB contingency presenting at the conference, given that one of the hot-button topics dealt with divestment from companies working in Israel.

I was recently able to catch up with Dave via telephone to learn more about what "sustainable and responsible investing" means within an organization as large as GBPHB and also to

seek his advice for ordinary people in terms of wise investment. GBPHB is not "small potatoes." The total value of its
funds is over $21 billion as it administers retirement plans,
health and welfare benefit plans, programs, and investment
funds for more than 91,000 active and retired clergy and
lay employees of the United Methodist Church. Dave has
served with the general board for eighteen years. Prior to
joining GBPHB, Dave held a brief tenure at a management-
investment firm after wrapping up a seventeen-year career
with Shell Oil Company. The latter part of his time at Shell
included managing the company's pension assets. This is a
guy who knows his stuff!

When I first asked Dave what the phrase "socially responsible investing" implied to him, Dave quickly informed me that
the language has changed; responsible investing is still important, of course, but investment that is "sustainable" is critical.
When I pressed Dave on what the word *sustainable* meant in
terms of investment strategy, he explained that GBPHB is a
signatory to the United Nations Principles for Responsible
Investment, meaning that GBPHB has committed to evaluating every investment choice in the light of environmental,
social, and governance factors, not just based on potential
financial return on investment. Investment decisions also take
the Social Principles of the United Methodist Church into
consideration. For example, the general board will not invest
in companies that derive 10 percent or more of their revenue
from gambling or the production and sale of alcohol, adult
entertainment, tobacco, weapons, and the operation of private
prison facilities.

The general board lists all of its holdings on its website, in
essence inviting stakeholders to hold it accountable for making sure it is investing into companies where sound environmental, social, and governance practices intersect with United
Methodist values. Dave indicated that a number of folks do
take advantage of the opportunity and follow up if they spot
an area of concern. Not all questions raised wind up meriting
general-board action, but some do. When I asked Dave for
an example, he indicated that United Methodist Women
brought to GBPHB's attention that Hershey Corporation
was sourcing cocoa from West African countries that regularly

deploy child labor. GBPHB was able to negotiate successfully with Hershey to bring about change. The Hershey Bliss line of candy is now made from fair-trade cocoa. By 2020 the company has committed to switching to all certified fair-trade chocolate.

In addition to its regular portfolio of investments, GBPHB also created a Positive Social Purpose (PSP) lending program in 1990 that works through qualified lending partners to make mortgage loans available to real estate projects that support low- and moderate-income individuals, families, and communities. Dave noted as we spoke that the mission statement of the United Methodist Church is "to make disciples of Jesus Christ for the transformation of the world." The general board's PSP program and sustainable investment practices are essential components toward accomplishing that mission.

I asked Dave for his best advice for ordinary individuals who might feel overwhelmed on what it means to be a responsible investor. Dave could relate to the question. "The folks that the general board serves are typically very smart people, often with advanced degrees, who are completely dedicated to their call. But often, they neither have the desire nor the time to acquire the financial knowledge needed to make optimal investment decisions." He continued, "I always warn people to be wary of anyone who approaches them with the opening gambit of 'Trust me.' There are many unscrupulous people out there who can and will take advantage of you." Dave, of course, recommended seeking wise counsel from trusted professionals. He also mentioned a number of trustworthy investment companies with strong reputations who "focus on the right things," including Calvert, PAX World, Trillium Asset Management, and Walden Asset Management.

The bottom line from Dave? Invest. It matters. It's important. But "investor beware."

7

Taxes and the Common Good

The word *taxes* is a highly charged and loaded word for many people. The connotations tend to be negative to almost anyone I have ever asked. As I researched this topic one day I idly Googled "most hated government agency." Two results seem to win by a landslide, TSA and IRS, and I suspect TSA was largely a post-911 addition to the "dislike" list. The IRS has no doubt been at the top of the dislike list in some form or another since the agency's inception in its earliest form in 1862. (It didn't pick up the name Internal Revenue Service until 1918.)

Ginghamsburg Church, where I have served as lead pastor since 1979, is located in a largely conservative district, and current Speaker of the House of Representatives John Boehner is its congressional representative. That being said, Ginghamsburg's congregation itself can be politically diverse. One weekend during my sermon a few years ago, I asked congregants to indicate by a show of hands, if they were willing, to share their primary political affiliation. The point of the message was to demonstrate how our allegiance to kingdom-of-God priorities supersedes that of any earthly political entity. The raised hands revealed Republicans, Democrats, Tea Party affiliates,

Libertarians, and so on. Although these disparate constituencies could find common ground in Jesus, I am not so confident they would find a common viewpoint on tax policy.

Most people have some sort of complaint about taxes, whether they feel citizens are taxed too much or they simply disagree about how the government is spending the money. More than half of our survey respondents had such complaints, 16 percent saying they "support lower taxes, period," and 42 percent saying they would feel OK about paying taxes "if they were better spent." These complaints have frequently led to demonstrations and revolts over the centuries. Wikipedia's article on tax resistance (incomplete and unverified as we know this crowd-sourced encyclopedia to be) listed 236 historical examples dating just from the first century AD through to the present—and we know via other historical sources that resistance to taxes didn't just start after the birth of Jesus.[1] Let's face it—people have never enjoyed paying taxes. Let's look at a few of the most well-known examples.

Although it is now believed that many of this story's details are legend versus fact, the story of Lady Godiva's tax resistance has been featured in both literature and film for centuries. Lady Godiva was an actual eleventh-century noblewoman who was married to a man named Leofric, the Earl of Mercia and Lord of Coventry. The historical Godiva was very generous to the church and with her husband helped to found a Benedictine monastery in Coventry. According to the legend, Lady Godiva was appalled by the heavy tax burden that her husband had placed on the citizens of Coventry. When she attempted to intervene with Leofric, he quipped that he would reduce the taxes only if she rode nude on horseback through the center of town. Allegedly, Godiva then stripped off her clothes, and using only her long hair to shield herself, galloped on a horse through the market square. Also, according to legend, she ordered the people to stay inside their homes and not to watch. All complied, except for one "peeping Tom," who was struck blind. But that story is a whole legend in itself. The Lady Godiva legend indicates that Leofric dutifully reduced

the taxes after the ride. Although the whole nude ride through
Coventry is historically suspect, taxes were clearly a concern in
the era. The legend was first documented just a hundred years
following the alleged horse ride.[2]

Moving ahead about seven centuries, we reach American
soil and the infamous Boston Tea Party. Before the birth of
the United States, when the original thirteen colonies were still
ruled by Great Britain, the British Parliament passed the Tea
Act of 1773, increasing import duties on tea shipped into the
colonies. In protest, merchants in some American cities refused
to accept incoming tea shipments. However, Boston merchants
ignored pressure from American patriots and allowed the tea to
enter the Boston Harbor. On the chilly night of December 16,
1773, about a hundred patriots, known as the Sons of Liberty
and under the leadership of Samuel Adams, disguised themselves as Mohawk Indians, boarded the merchant ships, and
jettisoned forty-five tons of tea. There was so much tea it took
them nearly three hours to complete the job. In today's dollars,
the tea would have been valued at almost $1 million. That was
one expensive protest![3]

Today's Tea Party movement in the United States, which
borrowed its name from this historic protest and uses the T.E.A.
acronym "Taxed Enough Already" as a slogan, has named fif-
teen nonnegotiable core beliefs. Not surprisingly, two of those
beliefs deal with taxes:

- Reducing personal income taxes is a must.
- Reducing business income taxes is mandatory.[4]

What is the saying? The more things change the more they
stay the same?

A more recent famous example of tax protest was Mohan-
das Gandhi's Salt March in India in 1930. Once again, the
resistance was against the British Empire, which ruled India
at the time. Similarly to its passing the Tea Act, the British
government had passed salt acts that prevented Indians from
collecting for themselves or selling salt, a staple of Indian diets.

Instead they were forced to buy salt from the British, with each purchase including a hefty salt tax. On March 12, Gandhi and several dozen followers set out on foot from Gandhi's religious retreat and started a 240-mile trek to a coastal town on the Arabian Sea, where they planned to gather their own salt in defiance of the law. Many more Indian protestors joined the march over the course of the journey, with the crowd reaching tens of thousands by the time Gandhi reached the salt flats. British police, in an attempt to stop the illegal making of salt and squash the protest, had crushed the salt deposits into the mud. Undeterred, Gandhi managed to pick up a small lump of natural salt from the mud, thus breaking the law. This small act started additional protests in other coastal cities, and served as one of many protests and demonstrations that eventually led to India's independence in 1947.[5]

WHAT IS THE COMMON GOOD?

The second part of this chapter title, "the Common Good," may not have nearly the same negative connotations as that T-word, but perhaps it is also controversial in its own right. What is "common good"? How do you define it? Like "beauty" and "fairness," it often seems to rest in the eye of the beholder.

One dictionary defines it as "the advantage or benefit of all people in society or in a group."[6] The catechism of the Catholic Church deploys the following definition: "the sum total of social conditions which allow people, either as groups or as individuals, to reach their fulfillment more fully and more easily."[7]

How do you define "common good"? How is your definition affected by your politics? In a column for *Time* magazine, Jim Wallis, the president and CEO of Sojourners, noted that we need new dialogue in the twenty-first century about what common good is and how to pursue it: "Our politics have become so polarized and increasingly volatile; and our political institutions have lost the public trust. Few Americans today would suggest their political leaders are serving the common good." Jim goes on to suggest that "common good" has its origins in Christianity:

> An early church father, John Chrysostom (c. 347–407), once wrote: "This is the rule of most perfect Christianity, its most exact definition, its highest point, namely, the seeking of the **common good** . . . for nothing can so make a person an imitator of Christ as caring for his neighbors." Of course, all our religious traditions say that we are indeed our neighbor's keeper, but today people of every faith don't often actually say and do the things that their faith says and stands for.[8]

I don't agree with Jim on everything, but we do have significant common ground in this area. Many of us as Jesus followers proclaim that we should "love our neighbors as ourselves" as the purest form of serving the common good, but our actions, or perhaps lack thereof, belie our words.

I look to the words of Jesus for my definition of the common good. It certainly includes "to love one another," the new commandment that Jesus gave in John 13:34. We see a more robust picture of what the common good looks like in Jesus' mission statement in Luke 4, where he quotes the book of Isaiah. Jesus proclaimed he was anointed to "'proclaim good news to the poor, . . . proclaim freedom for the prisoners and recovery of sight for the blind, [and] to set the oppressed free'" (Luke 4:18–19). In Matthew 25:31–46, Jesus gave a list of what it means to serve the common good:

- Feed the hungry.
- Give water to the thirsty.
- House the stranger.
- Clothe the naked.
- Care for the sick.
- Visit the imprisoned.

Those are tall orders and a long list in a world that is now home to over 7.2 billion people. This is why the power of multiplication and collaborative effort is so critical. A single church can have an impact on its neighbors; churches in partnership with one another can have significant impact on their cities; churches in partnership with one another, other nonprofits, as well as local, regional, and national governments, can have an exponential impact on the world. We can do together much more than we can do apart.

It's at this point in the dialogue that the words "separation of church and state" have probably popped into your consciousness. That topic could be, and has been, an entire book of its own and is too broad for this context. However, we do need to look into Scripture and see how the Bible and biblical history view government structures and authority, as well as taxes.

THE BIBLE AND GOVERNMENT TAXATION

Let's first evaluate what Scripture has to say about the legitimacy of government. The Bible does not by any means appear to be against government. Paul in Romans 13:1 writes, "Let everyone be subject to the governing authorities, for there is no authority except that which God has established." Jesus himself acknowledged that earthly authority was "established" by God when he responded to Pilate during the trial preceding his crucifixion: "'You would have no power over me if it were not given to you from above'" (John 19:11).

Paul continues in Romans 13:2–5 with the theme of why believers are to acknowledge and obey the legitimacy of government:

> Consequently, whoever rebels against the authority is rebelling against what God has instituted, and those who do so will bring judgment on themselves. For rulers hold no terror for those who do right, but for those who do wrong.

Do you want to be free from fear of the one in authority? Then do what is right and you will be commended. For the one in authority is God's servant for your good. But if you do wrong, be afraid, for rulers do not bear the sword for no reason. They are God's servants, agents of wrath to bring punishment on the wrongdoer. Therefore, it is necessary to submit to the authorities, not only because of possible punishment but also as a matter of conscience.

A Scripture passage attributed to Peter, the "father of the faith," in 1 Peter 2:13–14 directs us to submit ourselves "for the Lord's sake to every human authority: whether to the emperor, as the supreme authority, or to governors, who are sent by him to punish those who do wrong and to commend those who do right."

As Jewish men, Paul and Peter were both members of a people often marginalized and mistreated by the ruling Roman Empire, yet both acknowledged that earthly governments are established, or at least permitted by God, and following Jesus meant submitting appropriately to human authority.

Now I don't believe that we are to blindly obey bad or discriminatory laws. God's law takes priority, and there is a place for civil disobedience, whether it's the civil rights movement or recent protests and arrests of United Methodist bishops demonstrating on behalf of immigration rights. Yet, in most cases, governments are essential toward serving the common good, and government authority needs to be recognized and respected. Let's drill more deeply into what the Scripture has to say more specifically about paying taxes to earthly governments.

First we need to acknowledge that tax paying was no more popular in Jesus' day than it is today. In fact, I would dare say it was far more abhorred. To fund its vast operations and empire, Rome needed money, and its conquered territories were a significant part of its funding scheme. Palestine, where Jesus lived, was no exception. Taxes included a water tax, city tax, tax on other commodities like meat and salt, road tax, house tax, and more.[9] The Jews of Jesus' day who served as tax collectors were particularly despised, really for two reasons. First, every time they appeared they were an unwelcome reminder of Jewish submission to Roman rule. In a sense they were viewed as traitors to their own people. Second, many were extortionists and swindlers, charging excessively in order to line their own pockets. Jesus no doubt raised eyebrows among fellow Jews by his oftentimes close association with tax collectors, chiefly Matthew, called to be one of Jesus' twelve disciples, and Zacchaeus of nursery-song "wee little man" fame—the chief tax collector who clambered up a tree to see Jesus as he walked by and later hosted Jesus for dinner, confessing his sins of extortion and promising to make full restitution.

The most well-known story of Jesus and taxes is recounted in Matthew 22:15–22; Mark 12:13–17; and Luke 20:20–26. In other words, three of the four Gospels document what Jesus had to say about taxes. In this case, the legalistic Pharisees, who hoped to trap Jesus into a misstep that would place him in significant trouble with Roman authorities, sent some of their disciples, along with Herodians, to ask Jesus a question. Now, this was an interesting alliance. Pharisees, like many Jews, were not fans by any means of the Romans. Herodians, on the other hand, politically supported King Herod Antipas, a Jewish puppet king for the Romans. By extension then, Herodians were also supporters of Roman rule. Perhaps the only commonality uniting these two groups at this point in time was their distress over and desire to get rid of Jesus. The Pharisees' disciples and the Herodians approached Jesus with the following question: "'We know that you are a man of integrity and that you teach the way of God in accordance with the truth. You aren't swayed by others, because you pay no attention to who they are. Tell us then, what is your opinion? Is it right to pay the imperial tax to Caesar or not?'" (Matt. 22:16–17). In response, Jesus asked them to show him an example of the type of coin that would be used to pay the taxes. Someone handed him a coin known as a denarius, and Jesus continued the conversation in verses 20 and 21:

"Whose image is this? And whose inscription?"

"Caesar's," they replied.

Then he said to them, "So give back to Caesar what is Caesar's, and to God what is God's."

In both word and action, Jesus demonstrated that followers are to give to government any taxes owed. The apostle Paul reemphasized in Romans 13:5–7, "Therefore, it is necessary to submit to the authorities, not only because of possible punishment but also as a matter of conscience. This is also why you pay taxes, for the authorities are God's servants, who give their full time to governing. Give to everyone what you owe them: If you owe taxes, pay taxes; if revenue, then revenue; if respect, then respect; if honor, then honor."

CHRISTIANS AND THE ROLE OF GOVERNMENT

Let's evaluate current worldviews on taxes. In the United States, those who define themselves as liberals and those who define themselves as conservatives can espouse wildly varying stances. There are not completely black-and-white belief systems when it comes to taxes; there are many nuanced shades of gray between both ends of the spectrum. But in general, the more liberal viewpoint would embrace higher taxes on the whole than conservatives would, especially when it comes to taxing the wealthy. The more liberal worldview would claim that a high-enough tax rate is necessary for a large government to be able to create jobs, support welfare programs, and in general care for the poor and needy.

Conservatives on the other hand are more likely to promote lower taxes and a small government. The underlying belief would be that lower taxes give the common woman or man more opportunity and incentive to work, save, invest, and build their own lives. A pure conservative might see government programs as enabling dependency rather than empowering people to change their own lives.

From my perspective both sides make some valid points, but I also think neither alone has the complete picture. I believe governments must be strong enough and well-funded enough to serve the common good (though that does not let us off the hook as individual Jesus followers or faith communities). Yet empowerment, not enabling, must always be the core motivation underlying service to the common good.

God does expect governments to serve the poor and be conveyers of justice throughout Scripture. Let's return to Paul's words in Romans 13:4: "For the one in authority is God's servant for your good. But if you do wrong, be afraid, for rulers do not bear the sword for no reason. They are God's servants, agents of wrath to bring punishment on the wrongdoer." In this verse Paul references two of the primary roles of those in authority, those who govern: to be a "servant for good," or the common good, as well as to protect, addressing violence, crime, and safety for its citizens.

God's holding governments accountable for governing, ruling, and judging justly is a common theme throughout the Old Testament. Amos, in particular in chapters 1 and 2, describes the nations that will be destroyed because of enacting unjust policies and perpetrating unjust actions both domestically and internationally. Elsewhere in the Old Testament, prophets hold kings accountable for honoring God's priority toward care of the poor. The prophet Jeremiah, speaking of King Josiah, one of the good kings of Judah, said, "He defended the cause of the poor and needy, and so all went well" (Jer. 22:16). Psalm 82 is believed to be directed toward court magistrates, who were chastised by the psalmist and called to

> "defend the weak and the fatherless;
>   uphold the cause of the poor and the oppressed.
> Rescue the weak and the needy;
>   deliver them from the hand of the wicked."
>   (Ps. 82:3–4)

Psalm 72 opens with prayer for political leaders or kings, saying,

Endow the king with your justice, O God,
    the royal son with your righteousness.
May he judge your people in righteousness,
    your afflicted ones with justice.

May the mountains bring prosperity to the people,
    the hills the fruit of righteousness.
May he defend the afflicted among the people
and save the children of the needy;
    may he crush the oppressor.

(Ps. 72:1–4)

God holds those in authority accountable for being part of the solution toward care of the poor and needy. Some who disagree with this conclusion argue that care for the poor should be left to nonprofits, faith-based organizations, and churches. They will point out the myriad of food pantries that seem to exist on almost every corner or in every church basement of any struggling community. However, the numbers just don't add up. In the United States, federal nutrition programs provide twenty times more food assistance than churches or charitable programs. The government spent $102.5 billion in 2013 versus a charitable investment of $5.2 billion. It takes a collaborative effort.[10]

Most respondents to our *Christian Wallet* survey seem to agree that the answer is not either/or but both/and. Asked who should be responsible for assisting the poor (and allowed to mark all answers with which they agree) 83 percent said "communities and neighbors, personally caring for those in need," while nearly as many—81 percent—said it was the church's job, funded by member tithes and offerings. Even so, a full two-thirds said assisting the poor is also the job of the government, funded through our tax dollars. Twenty-one percent said the poor must be responsible for their own welfare, but if you do the math, you'll see that at least some of those respondents must have marked another option as well. Personal responsibility and our responsibility to care for those in need are not mutually exclusive.

Some might argue that it's fine for the government to provide some care for the poor and hungry inside our borders but decry expenditures beyond the United States. A poll conducted in 2013 revealed that Americans commonly think that 28 percent of the U.S. budget goes to foreign aid, which would make international aid a bigger expense than defense or social security. I frequently see this belief erringly touted on social media. In actuality, *less than one percent* of the U.S. budget is set aside for international aid outside of military-related support.[11]

We are all God's children and should all be fed, regardless of the accident of latitude and longitude of our birthplaces as we talked about in a previous chapter. Ginghamsburg Church's first investment into Darfur, Sudan, in 2005, was to create a sustainable agricultural program. Food insecurity was a vast and life-threatening issue since violence had prevented crops from being planted the previous growing season. Although our investment through God's miraculous multiplication put 5,209 Sudanese families back into the farming business, feeding approximately 26,000 children, women, and men, many would have starved to death before the new crops were harvested had it not been for the intervention of USAID. I think about that each spring when I sit down with my financial advisor to file my taxes.

Of course, to "uphold the cause of the poor" includes more than simply feeding the hungry. I was reminded of this when I read an article this past winter in my local newspaper titled "Many Still Struggling to Get Heating Help." I take my ability to set my thermostat where I will stay comfortable in January's chill for granted. It is easy for us to become isolated within our affluenza. Others are not so fortunate. The cost to support Dayton-area energy consumers needing utility assistance to keep their homes warm in the winter almost doubled from 2010 to 2014. Phone lines for the heating assistance program were overloaded with many struggling to get through in January 2015 when the article was published. The program is largely paid for by fees charged to individual utility customers.

But supplemental aid is provided through government funding. Federal money had already helped 60,000 people that winter receive a one-time emergency payment of up to $175 to avoid utility shutoff.[12] It takes all of us to keep people warm in the winter.

Care of the poor is not the only service that I believe is essential for governments to help provide with our tax investment. We mentioned Paul's allusion to government's responsibility to protect it citizens. We do need to defend ourselves from crime and terrorism inside our borders, as well as protect our country from outside, unwarranted aggression. Whenever I go through airport security and am asked to step aside to be patted down or have my bag checked, I can't say that I am thrilled about the slowdown, interruption, or perceived "invasion" of privacy. But I always take time to thank my bag checker for doing a good job. First of all, I am actually grateful for the safety that the individual is helping to provide via my tax dollars, but I also imagine that it can be stressful for that TSA agent to work for one of the most hated federal agencies next to the IRS.

I believe another key role that government tax dollars must help support is in the area of education. With many jobs having moved to newly emerging economies, it is important that we equip and retool students at home. I accessed the website for the Bureau of Labor Statistics, which had historically tracked job losses due to offshoring to find the latest statistics. Those statistics had been provided through a program called the Mass Layoff Statistics Program. Instead of finding numbers for 2014, I ironically found a notice that the tracking program had been eliminated in 2013 due to across-the-board federal spending cuts, commonly known as sequestration.[13] The U.S. Department of Commerce reported that "U.S. multinational corporations, the big brand-name companies that employ a fifth of all American workers . . . cut their work forces in the U.S. by 2.9 million during the 2000s while increasing employment overseas by 2.4 million."[14]

Although job losses have been somewhat extensive over the

past few decades as manufacturing moved to other countries, now the United States is starting to face a significant shortage of high- and medium-skilled employees, up to a projected 85 million by 2020. In 2013, 39 percent of U.S. employers were having trouble finding new employees with the right skill sets. At the same time, the United States is now ranked fourteenth in the world in its percentage of twenty-five–to–thirty-four-year-olds with some higher education.[15] We have also explored the troubling student debt statistics for those who do go to college. The resolution of this sticky situation will require all of us—students, parents, industry, and government.

In Ohio, schools are funded primarily via property tax, which creates school systems with huge inequities—another issue on which government will need to partner in resolving. State report cards for Ohio schools show a nearly straight-line correlation between poverty and state test scores. The wealthiest school system in Dayton, Ohio, had an enrollment of 4.69 percent of students living in poverty in 2012. Its student performance index score was 110.7. The school system with 94.05 percent of students living in poverty had an index of 75.5.[16] This does not sound like justice as the Old Testament prophets would have defined it.

Implementation and maintenance of our national infrastructure is also a crucial area for investment of tax revenue. In 2013, the American Society of Civil Engineers issued a report card giving U.S. national infrastructure an overall grade of D-plus.[17] Problem areas included drinking-water supply, aviation, roads, and sewage treatment. The ASCE concluded that it would require an investment of $3.6 trillion to restore it all to good working order by 2020. Furthermore, if the current level of spending continues, it will fall short of that figure by $1.6 trillion. The one area of infrastructure I imagine all of us have in common no matter where we live are our roadways, which received a D on the report card. This funding will need to come from somewhere and is unlikely to be supplied simply by private contributors.

Governments are also in the best position to regulate actions that are harmful to the common good and to ensure compliance with regulations that are designed to prevent or reduce them. Many of us may have concerns, sometimes valid, about the work performed by agencies such as the Environmental Protection Agency (EPA) or Food & Drug Administration (FDA), or about the scope of their authority. At the same time, I would hate to see what condition our water, air, and food supplies would be in without the protections regulated and enforced by these agencies. Taxes make the work of these regulatory bodies possible.

When looking at issues that directly impact both our Christian wallets and the poor, I am happy that federal regulators are finally addressing the payday loans industry. This $4.6 billion industry often preys on those who can least afford their services with exorbitant fees and "rollover" interest payments that can trap a borrower in a never-ending debt cycle. A recent Associated Press article profiled forty-year-old single mother Maranda Brooks, who took out a $500 loan to pay her electricity bill, agreeing first to a $50 fee. Two weeks later, she was surprised to see the full $550 deducted from her usual $800 paycheck, leaving her with little to feed her family of five. So Maranda was forced to take out another loan, the start of a debt cycle that lasted most of the next year.[18] Government regulation of industries that would otherwise operate only with their own profit in mind is essential for protecting the common good for all of us, especially folks like Maranda, who are most at risk.

JUSTICE FOR ALL

Scripture has a great deal to say about justice and fairness, and our taxes help run the governments that are to be key contributors toward making justice and fairness possible for all God's children. Government is one of the tools I believe God works through to accomplish God's purposes. My taxes are part of that mission. However, since justice and fairness for *all* is crucial, I also have no interest in government policy that mandates redistribution of wealth or exorbitant income tax percentage rates for those who do make above a certain income. Historically, Marxist governments that have tried to mandate like or equal outcomes for absolutely everyone have failed. First, because of human tendencies and corruption, they never achieve equal outcomes to begin with. Second, the attempt decreases incentives for people to be proactive producers of God's blessings either within their own or others' lives. We are designed to work and produce and to both enjoy and share the fruits of our labor. Proverbs 12:11 notes, "Those who work their land will have abundant food, but those who chase fantasies have no sense." Proverbs 10:4 shares the timeless truth that "lazy hands make for poverty, but diligent hands bring wealth." Our tax policies need to honor that truth.

We can provide tax relief and justice for the poor while not penalizing the successful, wealth-generating entrepreneur or investor. For instance, the Earned Income Tax Credit and Child Tax Credit assist low-income workers by increasing tax refunds. The former is credited with lifting seven million people, mostly children, out of poverty. Fairness and justice are not always easy, but they are possible.[19]

I am not an expert on government or tax policy, and this topic could expand into multiple books filled with voluminous research. But I do believe that taxes are part of God's plan and government has an important role to play. I also do not advocate blind acceptance of how our local, state, and national governments perform their jobs or spend our money. We need to stay informed in areas that touch our lives and livelihoods as well as those that affect social justice. We must be active voices and advocates for those lacking access and influence, and we should hold our governments accountable for contributing to, not limiting, ignoring, or destroying, the common good.

To wrap up this discussion on taxes and the common good, let's end with this wisdom from John Wesley's sermon "The Use of Money":

> "The love of money," we know, "is the root of all evil"; but not the thing itself. The fault does not lie in the money, but

in them that use it. It may be used ill: and what may not? But it may likewise be used well: It is full as applicable to the best, as to the worst uses. It is of unspeakable service to all civilized nations, in all the common affairs of life: It is a most compendious instrument of transacting all manner of business, and (if we use it according to Christian wisdom) of doing all manner of good. . . . it is an excellent gift of God."[20]

QUESTIONS FOR REFLECTION

- What positive results do you see from the taxes you pay?
- How can the church, other nonprofits, and the government work together to help those in need?

Meet Ambassador Tony Hall

I am proud to call Ambassador and Congressional Representative Tony Hall my friend. Tony, a Democrat, served in the U.S. House of Representatives from 1979 to 2002, representing the congressional district surrounding Dayton, Ohio. When leaving Congress, he was nominated by President George W. Bush to serve as the U.S. Ambassador to the United Nations Agencies for Food and Agriculture, a position he held until 2006. More recently Ambassador Hall worked on a Middle East peace initiative in collaboration with the Center for the Study of the Presidency. In this role, Tony once invited me to be part of a group of U.S. faith leaders who traveled to Israel-Palestine to work toward peace with Jewish, Muslim, and Christian sisters and brothers in Israel.

Tony first met Christ while serving in Congress, and that experience changed his life. However, even before committing his life to Jesus, Tony had a huge heart for serving the poor and hungry. He had observed the effects of extreme poverty while serving as a Peace Corps volunteer during the late 1960s in Thailand and later made alleviating world hunger a cornerstone of his life mission. Tony has traveled the world tirelessly working on behalf of the hungry. While in Congress, he fasted for twenty-two days in protest when the Select Committee on Hunger, which he chaired, was abolished. Tony also founded the Congressional Friends of Human Rights Monitors and the Congressional Hunger Center. I knew when it came to this topic of taxes and the common good, he was the right guy to approach.

When Tony and I recently spoke, I asked him about his commitment to the poor and hungry. What fueled his drive? Tony responded, "God is very clear that we are to be involved with the poor. If not, there would not be more than two thousand verses across both the Old and New Testament on that priority. Throughout Scripture we read about the oppressed, orphans, widows, and aliens." I then asked Tony a question that I knew from our previous conversations he frequently receives: "Aren't those Scriptures directed at believers? Isn't it the responsibility of believers to support the poor, not big government?" Tony almost interrupted me before I could finish the question. "True—it is believers' responsibility. But we need to face the truth—we don't give as we should, so the government has to step in." He then pointed out the statistics revealing that only about 9 percent of food relief comes from private sources, compared to the 91 percent supplied by the government. "The government has to step in."

I next asked Tony about his viewpoint on taxes. He reminded me of Jesus' directive in Mark 12:17 to render unto Caesar that which is Caesar's. Tony continued, "Our taxes are used to accomplish a lot of good. We have roads, we have sanitation systems, we can put our mouth to a faucet and drink the water. Our food is safe, and our laws help keep us safe." He also noted that our politicians often receive and sometimes merit a bad rap. Yet from his experience he can say without qualms that "for the most part our officials are clean and not corrupt. The people serving are good, and the government is good." Tony believes more people would be appreciative of the "goodness" of the U.S. government if they traveled to the places where Tony had been and experienced rampant, institutionalized corruption.

Tony went on to share more about the important services that government provides, ranging from defense to environmental protection. He reminded me of the story of the Cuyahoga River, which runs through Cleveland, Ohio, infamously known as the river that caught on fire—repeatedly—in the 1960s. A 1969 issue of *Time* magazine described the Cuyahoga as the river that "oozes rather than flows" and a river in which a person "does not drown but decays."[21] Tony noted, "No one took ownership of the problem or took any steps to stop the pollution and clean the mess up. The EPA had to step in and take significant action. Now you can fish out of that river." Tony pointed out that God has placed the sword of justice in government's hands and that is not to be taken lightly (Rom. 13:3).

Our leaders need our support to address the hunger and violence running rampant around the world, Tony said. For Jesus followers in particular, Tony pointed to key Scriptures in the Bible like 1 Timothy 2:1–2 that command us to pray for those who lead us. "We give it lip service. We pass over this text in the Scripture." He continued, "Government is an important part of God's structure, and if our leaders become corrupt, corruption starts to trickle down insidiously to all of us. Leaders have the power to make things good; leaders have the power to make things bad. We must commit ourselves to praying for our leaders at all levels of government."

Tony practices what he preaches. He has been meeting with a Republican colleague for prayer regularly for the past twenty-five years, and shared with me this thought: "Many politicians are lonely. Often they are not believers, or they may be afraid to let people get to know them—afraid that their flaws will be revealed. They need our friendship, and they need our prayers."

PART III

How We Live

8

Work to Live or Live to Work?

Last Friday evening I stopped at a liquor store on my way home from work to purchase a nice bottle of wine for a family celebration. As I approached the counter to check out, I greeted another customer with whom I had made eye contact as he placed a fifth of bourbon on the counter. "How're you doing?" I asked simply as a pleasantry. His response? "Fine, just trying to forget the work week." Too many of us in our TGIF and "Can't wait until I retire" culture end each week with that same sentiment. Contrast that attitude with a *Fast Company* interview with Jared Leto, in which the actor, investor, and entrepreneur said, "My work is never a job. My work is my life."[1] Where do we find the godly perspective between these two completely opposing viewpoints?

First of all, we can know from the account of the earliest days in the garden of Eden that God designed us for work, for laboring and producing fruits from what God has provided via creation. Genesis 2:15 notes, "The LORD God took the man and put him in the Garden of Eden to work it and take care of it." Psalm 128:2 assures us, "You will eat the fruit of your labor; blessings and prosperity will be yours." Solomon reminds us in Ecclesiastes 3:22, "There is nothing better for a person to enjoy their work. Because that is their lot." Of course, the Bible opens with God himself "working" as he creates planet earth and all of the creatures to inhabit it, and we find Jesus weighing in as we read in John 5:17, "'My Father is always at his work to this very day, and I too am working.'" Clearly "work" was not intended to be a four-letter word when viewed from God's perspective. Our work is meant to serve as part of God's divine plan for our lives and God's kingdom strategy.

Almost all of us who work do so in part because we need to have an income, some method for filling our Christian wallets so that we can spend, save, give, and invest with a conscience. Later in this chapter we will explore our attitudes about our incomes. But work is for a much larger purpose than simply bringing home a paycheck, whether it's the work we produce for our employment or the additional labor we invest simply for the kingdom. We ultimately work for the outcomes, not simply the incomes.

For many of us, we struggle to know how our work fits into the larger plan because we have never invested the time, prayer, and discernment into creating our life mission statement. We sail aimlessly through life without doing the hard work of attempting to define our life's God-sized purpose. In *Dare to Dream: Creating a God-sized Mission Statement for Your Life*, I describe how you can tell if a dream is from God: "It will always honor God, bless other people, and bring you joy. If it doesn't meet those three criteria, then it isn't a God dream, no matter how successful you are in accomplishing it. Success isn't the key here; significance to the Kingdom of God is."[2]

Some people who identify their life mission statements find that they can also pursue professional employment opportunities that are in close alignment with their God-sized purpose. Others cannot. Many people work jobs that seemingly do not align with their God dream at all but are necessary first and primarily to feed and shelter themselves and their families and then secondarily to provide resources for more expanded God deployment. Other folks don't even have the luxury of thinking about the latter.

SATISFACTION AT WORK

When I visited our first sustainable humanitarian project in Darfur, Sudan, in 2005, I met many women, typically widowed by the violence of the first genocide of the twenty-first century. They were struggling to raise multiple children in the hot, dusty, dangerous terrain and working extraordinarily hard to plant, tend, and harvest crops. There was nothing easy or glamorous about the work, and the outcomes were in no way guaranteed. But the work was necessary for survival, and yet somehow I saw in the women a sense of joy. They were grateful simply to have seed to sow, fields to toil over, and the opportunity to feed their children. We can learn something from the women of Darfur. Many of us need to find joy in our current employment and begin to discern the larger God purposes for the labor of our hands, heads, and hearts—no matter what our day job is. Perhaps if we renew our perspectives about our work, with an attitude of making an honorable and excellent offering to God, then God will expand our horizons. Our perspectives greatly influence our life outcomes.

As a pastor, I confess that it is easier for me to connect the dots between my paid employment and my life mission statement than it might be for many others. But I have not always been a pastor. As a college student at the University of Cincinnati, I worked as a cashier in a grocery store to pay for my tuition. I can still name a number of things I disliked about that position—especially the hours. My shifts frequently included Friday and Saturday nights as well as holidays, especially Thanksgiving. I couldn't wait to get another job. In the early days of my career as cashier, I had not yet realized that joy at work is far more dependent on attitude than circumstances. Before God could expand my influence and horizons, I needed a renewed attitude. Now, ironically, I find joy in working nights, weekends, and holidays like Christmas and Easter. But I had to learn to enjoy my work in the circumstances in which I found myself before God could use me in a more expansive opportunity.

Ecclesiastes 2:24–25 notes, "A person can do nothing better

than to eat and drink and find satisfaction in their own toil. This too, I see, is from the hand of God, for without him, who can eat or find enjoyment?" As Ecclesiastes 3:22 reminds us, "There is nothing better for a person than to enjoy their work." We see two key words in these Scriptures about God's plan for our work: *satisfaction* and *joy.*

I can identify three dimensions that God moves us through to find joy and effectiveness in our work. Each dimension takes us a little deeper than the one before. The first dimension God moves us through is leading us to understand that we *have* to work. If I don't work, I don't eat, and hunger is an incredible motivator. Work is God's gift to us as the means of provision for our daily needs. God has given me and you everything we need. He has given us soil, seed, sun, and rain. But the return on our harvest is in direct proportion to our investment of labor. Our return is based on how we maximize the gifts, the talents, and the time that God has given us.

Several years ago there was a short book that became extremely popular called *The Prayer of Jabez.*[3] The book was based on an obscure Scripture that most of us with theology degrees had never paid attention to in the past: "Jabez cried out to the God of Israel, 'Oh, that you would bless me and enlarge my territory! Let your hand be with me, and keep me from harm so that I will be free from pain.' And God granted his request" (1 Chron. 4:10).

What a great prayer! As I have noted, I find it my responsibility as a pastor to periodically remind those in my congregation that we are going to die. I am very aware of the limited number of years I have left on the planet to enlarge the influence of my harvest, to invest in that which will continue to live and expand beyond me. It is probably why my work week in my adult years has typically been six days in length. Most Americans work five days and rest two, which is fine. Yet Psalm 90:12 admonishes us "to number our days," God's reminder not to defer until tomorrow what we should invest our time and talents into today. You might agree with me that God's model is a pretty good plan. God worked for six days and rested on the seventh. Having a Sabbath is important and is even commanded. But I also remember my days are fleeting. I want to expand the territory of my influence; I want to see more people's lives transformed by Jesus Christ.

Initially as a cashier I complained about working nights and weekends. Now, with a transformed attitude, I have willingly through the years added Saturday-night and additional Sunday-morning worship celebrations to my weekend work. As we get older, it is not that we are to stop working, although the nature of our work or number of hours invested may be modified to accommodate our changing physical abilities. Or we may be financially able to move from paid employment to making significant unpaid contributions as a volunteer. No matter our age we need to understand that work is a gift from God and that the return on our harvest will be in direct proportion to the investment of our labor.

I see many Christians as they near retirement age move into comfortable complacency. I have some friends that talk more about their golf handicaps than their jobs. Yet retirement is not a widely espoused biblical concept. The only reference I have found to retirement is in Numbers 8:25, which indicates that the Levites were to retire at age fifty. (Fifty was about the maximum life expectancy at the time, however, so this rest was intended for those who lived an unexpectedly long time.) The rest of Scripture reminds us that from the beginning, "The LORD God took the man and put him in the Garden of Eden to work it and take care of it" (Gen. 2:15). We tend to compartmentalize our lives. We place the things we do for God in one bucket and what we do for our work in another. But Psalm 24:1 states, "The earth is the LORD's, and everything in it, the world, and all who live in it." We are here in a partnership with God to be part of the economic well-being of God's planet. Staying hungry is important.

A friend who is close to my age once shared with me that his plan was to have his house paid off while he was still in his fifties, which would also position him for early retirement. But a significant downturn in the stock market led to a significant decrease in his net worth as well as job loss due to a company's downsizing. He glumly shared with me right after it happened, "Now I *have* to work." It turned out to be the best thing that could have happened to him. Before then I had felt that my friend had gotten stuck in the 1980s. Even though we were roughly the same age, whenever I was around him he simply seemed old. He kept doing and saying the same old things with nothing new to share. After the job loss, when he had to pursue new employment and income, he gained a new lease on life. He became a learner again, rediscovered his creativity, and started two new businesses. When we stay hungry, we create new things and learn new ways. We are most like God when we are creating. Realizing we have to work can keep us fresh and creative. Work is our provision and our "creating" outlet. Haven't we all known people who spent years planning out in great detail all of their retirement hopes and dreams only to die within months or a few years of finally reaching retirement?

After acknowledging that we need to work, the second dimension in finding joy on the job is recognizing that we *want* to work. Work is about more than money, and our salary does not define our self-worth. Worth comes from the satisfaction and joy of making a productive contribution. Work even affects our physiological well-being. Ecclesiastes 5:12 says, "The sleep of laborers is sweet whether they eat little or much." Our work ultimately has little to do with how much money we make but everything to do with how we make a difference in the economy of God's garden. Whatever type of work we do, God has given us the privilege, with Jesus, to be part of God's redemptive work in the world. Institutional religion often creates this artificial barrier or box that declares that the only time we are doing God's work is when we are in church. This is not true at all. Everything we are about as Jesus followers is to be a part of God's redemptive purpose of the well-being and the economy of God's garden.

When I was in my late twenties, I met a man named Wally Ward. At age fifty-three, Wally had lost through bankruptcy a three-generation family business of apple orchards. Through this apparent "failure," Wally, a Harvard University graduate, discovered that his true passion was for traveling sales. When Wally was seventy-five-years-old, he and I had breakfast together at a local Tipp City diner. Even at seventy-five, Wally was still putting over 50,000 miles a year on his car making sales calls. His words to me over lunch that day are still branded in my soul: "I want to die waltzing past the receptionist, making my last sales call." Wally had clearly discovered the dance and joy of the gift of work.

Mikesell's Potato Chips is a Dayton-based company founded in 1910. Les Mapp, who had been named as the company's CEO in 1965, lived to the age of ninety-two. Up until the year before he died Les was in his office and on the job by 7:30 a.m. Les once shared with me that he actually felt that 7:30 a.m. was late; he had only succumbed to that late hour because of his advanced age. Les was a Christian, and he had met with me in my office at 4:30 p.m. one afternoon to talk about a mutual project. At that time of afternoon, most people are thinking about going home. Not Les. At the close of our conversation Les stood up and said, "Mike, I have to go back to my office and work on my long-range plan." At age eighty-four, Les was still committed to visioning forward and investing in his work. Like Moses at the end of his life, Les's "eyes were not weak nor his strength gone" (Deut. 34:7). To find joy on the job, we need an attitude adjustment: "I want to work." Then God will allow our influence and harvest to expand.

HONORING GOD IN OUR WORK

We reach the deepest dimension of right attitude toward our work when we can say, "I worship God through my work." Work is our greatest act of worship, and frankly it is where we spend the majority of our waking time. The Latin word for worship is the word *liturgy*, which literally means the work of God's people. All work should be God-centered work.

Scripture models this repeatedly. Part of Jesus' occupation was certainly Savior of the world, but he was also a carpenter. The apostle Paul was a tent maker. Neither Jesus nor Paul was paid to do what I do as a pastor, yet everything they did, both their "paid" work and unpaid efforts, was seamlessly integrated into the work of God. Their work was God-centered. Jesus said, "I only do what I see my Father doing" (John 5:19, paraphr.). If he were building a table as a carpenter, he would do it in the attitude of "I am doing the work of my Father who sent me." Not only did Jesus and Paul as carpenter and tent maker serve the purposes of God, they also provided care, products, and provision for people. Work is an act of worship, and God will use our work investment to enhance the lives of others.

Until my attitude was adjusted by serving as a grocery store clerk, God was not going to trust me to serve for the next forty years as a pastor. I had to learn that work wasn't simply about earning a paycheck; it was just as critically about serving people. In other words, I had to learn the importance of double bagging. I needed to expend extra time, money, and effort to meet the needs of people better. God is a God of excellence. As a Jesus follower, when I tackle my work with excellence, people are drawn to the contagious spirit of God's excellence within me. As a preacher, I still want to "double bag." All week long before I deliver a message, I spend hour after hour wrestling with God about the word I am supposed to bring that week to God's people.

Here is the second thing I had to learn as a cashier: never break the eggs. You have to be careful how you handle people through your work. Many of the customers I served were on food stamps. Cashiers tended to resent people on food stamps because it meant extra work for the cashier—more information to record and more hassle. It was easy to feel and demonstrate frustration, treating those customers as second-class. I had to learn to show grace and patience instead of irritation. Many times those folks would approach the counter and fall a few cents short. When I could, instead of requiring a customer to put a product back, I would go ahead and let the customer take the item, paying the shortage myself before the end of my shift so that my register would balance. Given that I made $2.35 an hour at the time, some of those shortages would take a bite out of my hourly income. But I learned over time that my work was not simply about me—it was about serving God and serving people. I wasn't just in the grocery business; I was in the God business.

A few years ago, Rev. Chris Heckaman, a United Methodist pastor and my supervisor at the time as our United Methodist district's superintendent, delivered the message at our main Tipp City campus over a Labor Day weekend. The thrust of Chris's message was on how to turn our TGIF into TGIM (Thank God it's Monday). As Chris pointed out, every sector in which we may be employed has an inherent God purpose if you take long enough to think about it. Manufacturing is about partnering as a cocreator with the Creator of all. Those who serve in the field of medicine often have a front-row seat to Jesus' healing power in action every day. Teachers and those who keep our schools running are working to raise up the next generation of servant leaders. And, of course, those in the service industry are working in the industry that is named after one of the most important words throughout the Bible. They are the folks who put the serve in service. Chris concluded his message by noting that our "profession is a key place for our profession—of faith," both through words and actions.

I realize that many people work in what can truly feel like thankless or difficult jobs. I do not want to minimize the challenges and frustrations that many face on a daily basis in their paid employment. I also believe, however, that in large part God places us into our specific work environments to fulfill a critical mission that is integral to all jobs—being salt and light to the customers and coworkers around us. In the Matthew 5:13–16 section of his Sermon on the Mount, Jesus told his listeners:

> "You are the salt of the earth. But if the salt loses its saltiness, how can it be made salty again? . . .

You are the light of the world. A town built on a hill cannot be hidden. Neither do people light a lamp and put it under a bowl. Instead they put it on its stand, and it gives light to everyone in the house. In the same way, let your light shine before others, that they may see your good deeds and glorify your Father in heaven."

As followers of Jesus, we are to bring the flavor of Jesus to our jobs. Salt dramatically seasons or enhances whatever it touches. As Christ followers, we are that transforming agent in our workplaces that brings out the best in whatever or whomever it infects. The light that emanates from us as we serve God and others excellently will expose the truth of who Jesus is to those with whom we come in contact. Ultimately, our words and actions will glorify and point others to God. Too often in the day-to-day grind we forget that we are to be the salt that brings out the flavor of the kingdom. Instead we adopt the flavorless or, worse yet, unsavory practices of the culture.

A fifty-three-year-old man in my congregation installs security systems for a living. It is a tough and often thankless job, physically demanding and with unpredictable hours. At the start of each early workday he has no way of knowing when the workday will end. It is dependent on the complexity of that day's installs, the whims of the clients, the cooperation of the technology, and the "on-hold" length of the tech-support hotline. It is stressful and challenging and not the job he would choose if another opportunity presented itself. Yet this man is a genuine and good-hearted Jesus follower. He cares about the quality of his work, and he cares about people, although those attributes make his days on the job even longer. I don't believe it is any accident that he also tends to be "randomly" assigned the most difficult customers—especially the elderly who are intimidated by the new technology and difficult to train and the newly widowed—grieving, lonely, and afraid of being in their homes alone at night after decades of marriage. If you were to ask this man, he would not see security-system installations as his life purpose. But it is at this point in life certainly his ministry. People understand who you are and whom you worship by the care, beauty, and quality of your work.

Whether we are pastors, cashiers, or security-system install-ers, I believe that God has created us to be successful in our work. But I also don't believe that God defines success the way the world tends to define success—by the size of our paychecks.

EARNING "ENOUGH"

As we have been exploring, this topic of work is much bigger than simply making money to fill our Christian wallets. The incomes we earn are also important. Most of us want to make more money than what it takes simply to survive. We also want to thrive, with resources left over to invest in the causes, places, and people we care about.

The U.S. government has established the poverty level for a family of four at an annual income of $23,850 within the forty-eight contiguous states.[4] The actual median house-hold income in the United States across all household sizes is $53,046.[5] Perhaps not too surprisingly, a Gallup survey con-ducted in spring of 2013 found that on average Americans think a family of four needs to make higher than either of those amounts, a minimum of $58,000 a year, just "to get by."[6]

Gallup also noted that perceptions of how much a family of four needs to make were not uniform across all Americans but were influenced by factors such as respondents' own income level, region of the country, and the community in which they lived, be it urban, suburban, or rural. Respondents who made more money thought everyone else needed to make more money as well. Suburbanites had higher expectations than rural or urban dwellers, and easterners (no doubt shaped by the high cost of living in many East-coast cities) typically named a higher income level for "just getting by" than their counter-parts in other regions. Gallup concluded, "Americans' percep-tions of what it takes to get by may, to a large degree, reflect their own lifestyles, rather than an objective assessment of local living costs."[7] Clearly there is a huge discrepancy between what Americans think they need to make and what the government claims they need to make.

Mark Rank, professor of social welfare at Washington University in St. Louis, says that almost everyone, no matter how much he or she makes, feels the need for at least a little more to live comfortably.[8] In our survey, 35 percent of respondents said they were "very satisfied" with the amount of money they earn at their jobs. Nearly half (49 percent), however, said they were "satisfied, but wish [they] made more."

In 2012, the Marist Institute for Public Opinions conducted a poll to see if there is a correlation between "happiness" and how much money people earn. They identified $50,000 as the happiness tipping point. "Respondents to the poll who made more than $50,000 were more satisfied with their lives concerning factors ranging from friends, to health, to how they spent their time." A 2010 Princeton University poll had identified $70,000 as the magic number.[9]

Part of our perceived happiness with our incomes seems to be based on what Learnvest.com calls "comparisonitis." In chapter 1 we identified it as keeping up with the Joneses. Apparently, we aren't happy when we compare our lifestyle to that of someone who makes much more money than we do. But we also get into trouble when we compare ourselves to someone in a worse financial position than we are. If our credit-card debt, for instance, is a third of that of our friends, we may tend to pat ourselves on the back and head to the nearest high-end, fresh-air shopping center for a "well-deserved" shopping spree.[10] Looking to others' financial circumstances to determine how happy we should be with our own is never a good idea.

Making money in and of itself is never a bad thing. If you feel like your employer underpays you, I recommend that you build your case and negotiate for a raise. Also, I encourage you to find new ways to earn additional income. As I share in *Dare to Dream*, assessing the gifts you already have of head, hands, and heart that could be deployed toward new income sources is a great starting point. Perhaps running an eBay store or doing odd jobs via a service like Taskrabbit may be just the ticket. But don't expect the additional money to buy you happiness, just opportunity.

A job well done, a satisfied customer, gratitude for what you already possess and the money you already make, the sense you are living out the impassioned purpose that God has planted deep in your heart—those are the circumstances that produce joy, not the size of your paycheck. Seek meaningful work that produces God-honoring outcomes, not just income.

If you are an employer, you also have a responsibility and an opportunity to help your employees experience more meaningful employment. Employee engagement is critical. A "State of the American Workplace Report" issued by Gallup in 2013 found the following:

> Organizations with an average of 9.3 engaged employees for every actively disengaged employee in 2010–2011 experienced 147% higher earnings per share (EPS) compared with their competition in 2011–2012. In contrast, those with an average of 2.6 engaged employees for every actively disengaged employee experienced 2% lower EPS compared with their competition during that same time period.

Gallup goes on to conclude that employee disengagement costs the United States $450-to-550 billion per year. Clearly, deeply engaged employees represent a win-win for both employee and employer. If you are an employer interested in increasing your employees' engagement, I recommend you take the time to order the study report at Gallup.com.[11]

Finally, a word of encouragement to the more seasoned among us—even if you have spent decades working in a position that has never felt quite aligned with your wiring or calling, it's never too late. *AARP, The Magazine* recently reported that registered nonprofits grew 21.5 percent from 2001 to 2011 and that approximately nine million people between ages forty-four and seventy currently work for social-purpose organizations as second careers or after retirement. I encourage you to start thinking about what might be your own "second acts for the greater good."[12]

Ultimately, we find satisfaction in our work when we live out the passions of our heart, not our materialistic desires. If God had not called me to be a pastor, I would have been a teacher or a social worker. None of these professions has ever been considered a wealth generator, but they certainly reflect my sweet spot. I have to be true to my calling. God has demonstrated to me again and again that when I wisely deploy my Christian wallet when I chase the mission and not the money, the money follows.

QUESTIONS FOR REFLECTION

- Do you find your work meaningful and/or enjoyable, or is it just a paycheck?
- Do you feel satisfied with the amount you earn? Is it "enough"? If not, how much more do you feel you would need to live comfortably?

Meet the Foglemans

I have never met Drs. Lynn and Sharon Fogleman, ages fifty-nine and sixty-one, in person, but I am a huge fan. Our long-distance relationship started in 2014 when a missions' team from Ginghamsburg Church visited Yei, South Sudan, to bring back the story of how our Imagine No Malaria funds were being deployed to save lives in the region. Sharon and Lynn were also in Yei, working in community health education and disease prevention in partnership with the United Methodist Church.

By no means was South Sudan their first place of missional deployment. The couple, who have been married for thirty years, served in medical missions in Maua, Kenya, for a decade starting in 1987. From 1997 to 2011, before moving to South Sudan, they practiced medicine at the Red Bird Clinic in Beverly, Kentucky, a distressed mountain community isolated in a rugged region of the Appalachians.

It's not like Lynn and Sharon do not have other options. Lynn earned his MD from the University of Kansas School of Medicine in 1980 and then completed a family-practice residency. Sharon graduated from the University of Iowa College of Medicine in 1982 and completed her family-practice residency in 1985. Both felt deeply called to be doctors. Sharon noted, "Back in the 70s, it was still unusual for a woman to go into medicine, and I had never met a woman physician until after starting med school. But I was raised to believe that I could do anything that I wanted to, and God kept putting the idea into my head and heart, despite the fact that it took me three attempts to get accepted into medical school." Lynn, after exploring and discarding several college majors, concluded that he wanted to go into a profession where he could "more easily demonstrate my love for Christ." Medicine made that possible.

Both Lynn and Sharon had their first significant mission experiences as medical students. Sharon spent time serving in the Dominican Republic, Sierra Leone, and Haiti, and Lynn had his own experiences in the Dominican Republic. In fact, he and Sharon, single at the time, were both part of the same trip. Lynn noted, "After experiencing a hint of the life of service in medical missions in a developing country, and after viewing my own culture in a different light upon my return, I knew in my heart that this was what I must do. I could not remain in my own land of excess while people who had so little access to medical care did without." And the rest, as the saying goes, was history.

Clearly, Lynn and Sharon are not working for the income, but for the outcome. In Kenya, their income was approximately 20 percent of what they could have made in family practice stateside. At Red Bird Clinic, they "shared a position," which brought in a salary reflecting approximately 75 percent of what one have them could have made in a typical medical practice. To serve in South Sudan, they raise their own support and have a combined salary of $37,000. So why do they do it?

Lynn shared this in a recent e-mail: "We believe that our treasure is where our heart is, and our heart needs to be centered on Christ. Things and money get in the way of what is eternally valuable. We also believe that the excess-mentality of our culture is an offense to God. Our materialistic excess attempts to replace God as God, and so many resources wasted simply on ourselves makes less available to care for the needs of God's people. We intentionally choose to live simply so that others may simply live."

The Foglemans would not, however, describe themselves as self-denying saints. It doesn't take them long to rattle off the benefits of their career decisions. First, their lifestyle positioned them to model and demonstrate biblical money matters and right kingdom priorities for their three children. Their simpler lifestyle has also meant no mortgage, no credit-card debt, and no keeping up with the Joneses, while instead providing incredible travel opportunities and deeply rich life experiences. The Foglemans have also learned how to accept the generosity of others. Sharon noted, "Raising our salary and ministry funds can be *very* humbling. But we have the joy of hearing how God blesses those who give toward the mission. Our need becomes an opportunity for others to give."

Asked her advice on meaningful work, Sharon asks a few questions of her own: "Does your work engage you, draw you in deeper, challenge you to grow? Does it contribute to the benefit (and not the detriment) of life for human beings and God's creation? Ending each work day with a clear conscience and a peace-filled soul—that's our definition of true success."

Most people I meet who are the Foglemans' age are seeking retirement; Lynn and Sharon are avidly pursuing God's mission.

9

Choosing Our Neighbors

In late spring 2013, many of us were glued to our TVs or news-feeds as the story of Ariel Castro unfolded. Between 2002 and 2004, Castro had kidnapped three young girls and held them captive in his Cleveland, Ohio, home for roughly a decade, fathering a child with one of them. In May 2013, one of the prisoners, Amanda Berry, managed to escape with her six-year-old daughter and contact the police, finally bringing the ordeal to an end. After the women's imprisonment came to light, Ariel Castro's neighbors wound up sharing with one another some troubling and unusual things they had observed over the past ten years. Despite noticing something was "off" about the man and his home, no one had talked with other neighbors, confronted Ariel, or acted to investigate further.

A columnist for the *Washington Post* writing about the Castro story, Peter Lovenheim, reflected back on an incident when he and his family had lived on a suburban street in Rochester, New York. A man who had lived in the neighborhood for seven years, ten houses down from the Lovenheim family, came home one night, shot and killed his wife, and then turned the gun on himself. Their two children ran out of the house screaming. Lovenheim noted,

> I didn't know the family well, and in asking around, I found that no one else did, either. Much like in Cleveland, there had been some warning signs that became much brighter in hindsight: A few weeks earlier, a neighbor saw a police car in the driveway; a close friend suspected that the husband had purchased a rifle; another neighbor thought the husband's behavior had recently seemed 'off.' But everyone kept their bits of information to themselves, and on the night of the shooting, we were all shocked.
>
> I wondered: Did I live in a true neighborhood or just on a street surrounded by people whose lives were entirely separate from my own?[1]

That's a great question! How well do we know our neighbors? I realized about a year ago that I didn't know mine very well at all. I am the pastor of a megachurch and passionately evangelistic. Yet last spring I had a knock on my door from an eighth-grade neighbor who lives on the same seven-house cul-de-sac that Carolyn and I do. She asked me a pointed question: "How can I get my family to come to your church?" She went on to explain that the family had attended Ginghamsburg Church that Easter and really enjoyed it, finding our band's rousing rendition of Pharrell Williams's "Happy" a highlight. However, the family had not been back. Talk about a challenging question! Here I am, a four-decade-plus pastor, a nearly five-decade Jesus follower, and my young neighbor had to approach me about inviting her own family to my church. Ouch. Carolyn and I are now working much more intentionally to know our neighbors. And my young neighbor's family has become very active at Ginghamsburg over the past year.

Throughout my Christian life, I have always spent Holy Thursday engaged in some type of spiritual experience with fellow Christians. This year, Carolyn and I did something completely different, and I encouraged the rest of the church family to do so as well. We invited all of the neighbors who live on our cul-de-sac to our home for hors d'oeuvres and wine. Twelve people were able to come, and we had a wonderful evening together. I am embarrassed to report that one couple, who had built their home in the neighborhood at roughly the same time we had—twenty-two years ago—we were basically meeting for the first time. Two other neighbors who came to our gathering had lived in the neighborhood for fourteen and twenty-one years, respectively. They recognized each other—from seeing each other at the local Catholic church—never realizing until that night that they were neighbors.

The isolation in which we are all going about our lives is disheartening. My original focus for this chapter was the way in which we isolate ourselves socioeconomically, so many of us choosing to live far away from possible interaction or community with the poor. This isolation debits both the richness of our own lives as well as the lives of those who live in poverty. That's an important topic that we will explore later in the chapter. But, as my Holy Thursday experience revealed, many of us are living in isolation from our neighbors, regardless of where our homes may be physically located. It is the relational poverty that kept me from inviting my own neighbors to my own church and that allowed an Ariel Castro to hold three precious lives hostage for more than a decade.

WHO IS MY NEIGHBOR?
NO, REALLY—WHO IS HE?

Maclean's magazine reported in 2014 that approximately 50 percent of Americans didn't know their neighbors' names, 30 percent of Canadians felt "disconnected from their neighbors," and a poll of two thousand British citizens found one-third declaring that they would be unable to pick their neighbors out of a police lineup.[2]

Lovenheim in his *Washington Post* column summarized the various reasons sociologists provide for this "side-by-side" isolation:

- Two-income families result in fewer people at home during the day.
- More time is spent on television and using the Internet.
- Suburban lot and house sizes increase physical distances between homes.
- Fences around yards have become a standard feature.

Lovenheim also points out that in previous generations the word *stranger* primarily identified a person we hadn't yet met. Today, the connotative association with the word *stranger* is "threat." It's no wonder that "community" within our communities is so quickly becoming a relic from our parents' and grandparents' generations.[3]

God has designed us to live in close community with one another—not to live in isolation. We will explore that scripturally in a few moments. But scientific evidence also supports this innate need for community. In 2013, *Slate* magazine reported the physiological consequences of loneliness from a number of medical studies. The impacts are astounding:

- The elderly who live in social isolation are twice as likely to die prematurely. Their increased mortality rate was comparable to that of smoking.
- Loneliness is approximately twice as dangerous to our health as obesity.
- Social isolation can lead to diabetes, heart disease, and arthritis because it impacts the immune system.
- The lonely don't sleep as well; they are more likely to experience microawakenings, which might suggest the brain is on higher alert for threats throughout the night.[4]

We need to know and engage with our "neighbors." First, God commands it, and second, we ourselves need community for our own health and well-being.

We are directed eight times in Scripture to love our neighbors. One of the first appears in the book of Leviticus, the book of rules, regulations, and guidelines that taught God's people how to live godly lives: "Do not seek revenge or bear a grudge against anyone among your people, but love your neighbor as yourself. I am the LORD" (Deut. 19:18). The theme is then frequently repeated in the New Testament, credited in four passages to Jesus in the Gospels as well as echoed by Paul in the book of Romans and Galatians and by James, often thought to be Jesus' brother, in his own epistle. When an expert in Jewish law asked Jesus what is the greatest commandment, Jesus responded, "'Love the Lord your God with all your heart and with all your soul and with all your mind." This is the first and greatest commandment. And the second is like it: "Love your neighbor as yourself." All the Law and the Prophets hang on these two commandments'" (Matt. 22:37–40). Paul stated that the "entire law is fulfilled in keeping this one command: 'Love your neighbor as yourself.'" (Gal. 5:14). Loving our neighbors clearly isn't a choice to be made but a mandate to follow.

Let's examine how and where Americans live. The U.S. Census Bureau indicates that 80.7 percent of the U.S. population lives in urban areas. This includes city dwellers as well as most suburb dwellers. It defines as "urban" both urban clusters and urban centers. Cluster populations range between 2,500 and 50,000 people. An urban center is any area with a population of over 50,000. Only 19.3 percent of Americans live in rural areas as defined by the Census Bureau. However, living in a densely populated urban center may not necessarily mean less social isolation.[5]

In 2012, the bureau issued a report titled "America's Families and Living Arrangements: 2012," identifying some interesting shifts. Report highlights included the following:

- Sixty-six percent of households in 2012 were single-family households, down from 81 percent in 1970.
- Between 1970 and 2012, the share of households that were married couples with children under eighteen halved from 40 percent to 20 percent.
- The proportion of one-person households increased by

10 percentage points between 1970 and 2012, from 17 percent to 27 percent.

- Between 1970 and 2012, the average number of people per household declined from 3.1 to 2.6.
- Black children (55 percent) and Hispanic children (31 percent) were more likely to live with one parent than non-Hispanic white children (21 percent) or Asian children (13 percent).
- During the latest recession, homeownership among households with their own children under the age of eighteen fell by 15 percent. These households saw a 33 percent increase in parental unemployment.
- Multigenerational households are less common among whites and most common among African Americans and Hispanics. Those multigenerational households are more likely to be living in poverty.

Household sizes are shrinking; more people are living alone; the recession is decreasing household stability; and minority children are more likely to live in single-parent or multigenerational homes. While it is a cultural norm in many places around the world to live with extended family and multiple generations under one roof, in the United States today the most common type of multigenerational household consisted of a householder living with a child and a grandchild, often for economic reasons. Other trends noted were an increased likelihood that those aged eighteen to thirty-four would live in their parents' home than would have done so back at the turn of the millennium. On a less than optimistic note, the report concluded, "The economic well-being of all family types worsened on average in the 2007–2009 recession and in the years since its official end."[6]

In my research for *The Christian Wallet*, I discovered several sources in 2014 reporting that Millennials (those able to move out from their parents' homes) were choosing to leave suburbia and move to urban centers. The *New York Times* reported that the "number of college-educated people age 25 to 34 living within three miles of city centers has surged, up 37 percent since 2000, even as the total population of the neighborhoods has slightly shrunk."[7] Yet this attraction to more densely populated areas does not mean young people will necessarily form lasting bonds with their neighbors; a report from Trulia.com in early 2015 indicated that urban dwellers were less likely to want to be living in the same area in five years than those currently living in the suburbs or rural areas.[8]

Breaking out of these new norms of isolation requires intentionality and sometimes a countercultural mind-set: planning weekly meals with another family, relocating to live next door to close friends or family members, even sharing a home with another family. When Ari Weisbard and his wife bought a house jointly with another couple, other friends were shocked, even more so when they learned the other couple was expecting a baby. Weisbard sees a lot of value in their arrangement, however, and says he hopes they will all live and raise their children together in that house for decades.[9]

"While most people take for granted that dual-parent households usually have more resources to deal with life's challenges than single parents, why stop there?" Weisbard says. "By forming a household with friends who share our values, we realized we could build an even stronger system of support than we would have in separate homes."

Stories like that seem few and far between, however, with most of us choosing more privacy, when possible, and quite often isolating ourselves not just from our neighbors but from anyone "not like us."

SEGREGATING OURSELVES

What concerns me the most as I reflect on the topics of community and isolation is how America seems increasingly to be a nation of great divides. We remain too divided in terms of race decades after the passage of the civil rights agreement. Discrimination based on sexual orientation is threatening to split churches and communities. We are deeply divided over immigration and U.S. border-control policy. Across the board, politics are increasingly rancorous and unproductive. The Pew Research Forum issued the report "Political Polarization in the American Public" in July 2014. Perhaps not too surprisingly Pew noted that ideological division between Republicans and Democrats was deeper and more extensive than at any point in the last two decades. The report indicated that a large percentage of party members from both sides went beyond simply "disliking" the other party, with 27 percent of Democrats and 36 percent of Republicans seeing the opposing party as an actual "threat to the nation's well-being."[10]

Interestingly, this political divide also influences whom we choose as neighbors. Political polarization begins at home as our choices of where to live lead to self-segregation by politics and other demographics. The aforementioned Pew report states, "People with consistently conservative views overwhelmingly favor small towns and rural areas as places to live: 41% say they'd live in a rural area if they could live anywhere in the U.S., while 35% pick a small town. Conversely, 46% of people with consistently liberal views say they prefer to live in cities. (About two-in-ten of those in every category choose the suburbs.)" Partisanship is also associated with the value we place on ethnic diversity when choosing where we want to live. According to Pew, "76% of consistent liberals said racial and ethnic diversity was an important factor in deciding where to live, compared with just 20% of consistent conservatives." The report goes on to note that consistent conservatives think a shared religion is more important when it comes to choosing our neighbors, to the tune of 57 percent.[11]

Perhaps the deepest divide of all is the gap between the economic haves and have-nots, which in turn is even wider when race is taken into consideration. The 2007 to 2009 recession was certainly a key culprit, but there has been tremendous inequity for quite some time that only accelerated during the recession. A Pew Research Forum report released in December 2014 noted that median net worth in U.S. households had decreased for all Americans from 2007 to 2013, but the decrease was most significant for nonwhite households. The median net worth for white households, which was $192,500 in 2007, dropped 26.3 percent to $141,900 in 2013. Hispanic median household net worth has long trailed after that of whites at only $23,600 in 2007, dropping 41.9 percent to $13,700 in 2013, far below a livable standard. The news was even more grim for African American families. In 2007 black household median net worth was about ten times less than white households at $19,200. By 2013, it was thirteen times less than white households, dropping to a dismal $11,000. This doesn't seem just to me.[12]

Current socioeconomic status greatly impacts children's futures. A study by Harvard University and the University of California at Berkeley examined the odds of a child moving up the economic ladder within the nation's one hundred largest economic centers. My state of Ohio did not fare so well. Dayton was ranked as 79th out of the top-one-hundred list in terms of opportunity for upward mobility, and a child whose parents were in the bottom 20 percent of income distribution has a mere 5.9 percent chance of rising to the top 20 percent of earners when he is an adult.[13] I am not a gambler, but those don't sound like great odds to me. Other major Ohio cities including Cleveland, Columbus, and Cincinnati fared even worse. Our tendency toward social isolation and self-segregation compounds these harsh realities. The study noted that in places where minorities, people in poverty, and those who are affluent are more isolated from one another, the prospects of poorer children are the worst. This isn't surprising, since public schools are typically funded by the taxpayers who live in that community, leading to better-funded schools for children of economically advantaged parents and struggling schools for children whose parents are too poor and less able to provide other opportunities.

I found a recent story in the *Washington Post* particularly heart-wrenching. A *Post* reporter interviewed Robert Putnam, the Harvard political scientist known for his book *Bowling Alone*. The interview preceded by a matter of days his newest "manifesto" titled *Our Kids: The American Dream in Crisis*. In short, Putnam is on a mission to make inequality of opportunity for kids a key theme in the 2016 presidential election. He identifies another widening gap between the haves and have-nots in terms of childhood opportunity for developing into new life pictures. The article notes, "Better off families are spending ever-more money on their children. They're volunteering even more at their children's schools. Their children are pulling away as Mary Sue [Putnam's representative name for a child living in poverty] falls further behind."[14]

The article posits that poor children aren't only lacking in material wealth; they are also significantly lacking in mentors. Many live with single parents and working-class adults who have lost job prospects and financial stability because of the recession and have little dedicated quality time for their offspring. Less-educated parents also tend to have and spend less time on reading to infants and toddlers, a key brain-development opportunity. The article indicated that poor children get forty-five minutes less than well-off kids every day of what Putnam calls *Goodnight Moon* time.

For those of us who are parents with the economic means and time to help our children do well, we know how bewildering it can be to help children choose the best academic courses in high school, select extracurricular activities that marry passions to what will look good on a college application, and actually complete the application submission process itself—much less fill out the dreaded FAFSA form early each new year to qualify for financial aid. How can the Mary Sues of the world compete? This is one reason why Ginghamsburg Church's Clubhouse program, and others like it, are so critical. It trains talented teens to serve as leaders and mentors and then places them in Clubhouses in at-risk communities to provide after-school care, mentoring, and homework help for children.

Putnam profiles two high school sisters he identifies as Lola and Sofia, who grew up in a poor, gang-ridden neighborhood of Los Angeles with no parents to speak of. A grandparent kept them on track for a period of time before she died as well. Lola and Sofia have had to navigate life without parents, tutors, coaches, and mentors of any kind. They perceive their teachers as disinterested, choosing to invest their energies instead into the "smart kids." When Lola attempted to join the reading club she was told she couldn't read well enough. Sofia learned that her grades weren't high enough for her to join the volleyball team. This is heartbreaking to me! Putnam describes Lola and Sofia's view of the world as a very lonely one.

Lola and Sofia and Mary Sue aren't the only ones who lose when communities are segregated by socioeconomic status. Those with the means to choose bigger homes and safer neighborhoods may find a different kind of poverty in their souls. Part of Putnam's research implied what some have dubbed the "money empathy gap," based on research implying that the more money you have the less humane you may tend to become.[15]

In Putnam's case, he returned to the town where he grew up in the 1950s, Port Clinton, Ohio, and studied his graduating class to see how well its members had done as a whole in upward mobility. For Putnam's generation, the results were astonishingly good. However, he noted in his research that the current working-class kids in Port Clinton were "locked into troubled, even hopeless lives." Needless to say, some Port Clinton residents perceived it as a wake-up call; others not so much. One mother from a wealthier Port Clinton neighborhood was wary of providing additional funding for poor kids. "'If my kids are going to be successful,' she said, '. . . I don't think they should have to pay for other people who are sitting around doing nothing for their success.'" Her comment demonstrates little-to-no empathy for the uneven, unfair playing field on which poor kids find themselves. Perhaps this mother is far too narrowly defining the "neighbor" she is called to love.

One of the biggest expenditures we make out of our Christian wallets is on our home. Let's make sure that as we choose the home that is right for our family, we do so with our values in mind, not chasing status or avoiding a perceived "threat," but desiring true community with our neighbors and success for all God's children.

AVOIDING THE "OTHER"

Christians in particular seem to choose isolation and segregation from the rest of the world God loves, narrowly defining "neighbor" as someone who looks like us, acts like us, and, most important, believes like us. As writer Scott Christian (his actual name) recently noted in a Religion News Service column, Christians seem to love to create Christian versions of everything, citing examples including music, book, and film festivals; TED talks; and even a Christian fashion week. Scott Christian warns, "While it might seem tempting for Christians to lock themselves away in anti-secular bubbles, where they could wear nothing but Christian clothing and eat nothing but Christian food (Chick-Fil-A, I'm guessing?), the ramifications of doing so are polarizing at best, and deeply destructive at worst."[16] I would have to agree! How can we be salt and light in the world when we refuse to touch the people and circumstances that would benefit from a little seasoning, or we won't take the spotlight beam off of ourselves long enough to shine the light of Jesus into the world's dark corners? An isolated Christian quickly becomes an impotent Christian.

As we noted in chapter 4, it's not just we as individuals who do not know our neighbors—our churches don't know their neighbors either. Too many of us commute to churches far from where we live, congregate only inside church walls, and leave most of our buildings' doors locked the majority of the week. We become the proverbial mausoleum for "saints" instead of the hospital for "sinners." If we look outward at all, too often it is a half-hearted attempt to coax the world into our churches instead of taking our churches into the world as the hands, feet, and voices of Jesus—as true "neighbors" to our neighbors.

Many of us also choose to avoid public school systems for our children, perhaps homeschooling instead or, if we can afford it, sending our children to private Christian schools. I am not opposed to either; I have seen remarkable and highly engaged young people emerge from homeschooled and private-school backgrounds. But I think it requires a robust effort on the part of their parents or guardians to ensure a private education equips students for the mission of Christ into the world and not for life-long seclusion and exclusion from a diverse group of neighbors.

Nearly half a century after Martin Luther King Jr. declared Sunday morning as "the most segregated hour in America," our churches still exist within a great racial divide. The Pew Research Institute reported in late 2014 that "about eight-in-ten American congregants still attend services at a place where a single racial or ethnic group comprises at least 80% of the congregation." Fortunately, that trend is slowly starting to reverse. Pew reported in 1998 that 20 percent of U.S. white churchgoers attended church services with absolutely no one of another race or ethnicity. By 2012 that percentage had dropped to 11 percent.[17] But there is still work to be done.

I am frankly more concerned about Christian attitudes toward segregation within our churches than I am relieved by the growth in diversity. A recent Lifeway research report, like Pew, noted that eight in ten U.S. congregations are made up of one predominant racial group. However, its survey also revealed that many churchgoers appear to be happy with the status quo. Here are a few of the salient points:

- Fifty-three percent of the study respondents disagreed with this statement: "My church needs to become more ethnically diverse."
- Forty-two percent felt their church was doing enough already to embrace diversity.

- Thirty-three percent strongly disagreed that their church needed to be more diverse.
- Seventy-one percent of those identified as evangelicals say their church is diverse enough.[18]

What is it within us that perpetuates this desire to be separate from those unlike ourselves both in our homes and in our churches? I wonder how many of us could only retort with the "Good fences make good neighbors" line, long memorialized in one of my favorite Robert Frost poems "The Mending Wall," if asked point blank. Yet if we truly claim to answer Jesus' call to "follow me," we no longer have the luxury of isolation from our sisters and brothers. We must broaden our definition of "neighbor."

Scripture makes it clear that diversity, of all types, is a kingdom value. On the birthday of the church, the day of Pentecost, the diversity of the known world was present: "Now there were staying in Jerusalem God-fearing Jews from every nation under heaven. . . . Parthians, Medes and Elamites; residents of Mesopotamia, Judea and Cappadocia, Pontus and Asia, Phrygia and Pamphylia, Egypt and the parts of Libya near Cyrene; visitors from Rome (both Jews and converts to Judaism); Cretans and Arabs" (Acts 2:5, 9–11).

God's priority on diversity and inclusivity is not just ethnically or nationally focused. One of Jesus' most instructive parables about who is kingdom material, so to speak, is the parable of the Great Banquet in Luke 14:15–24. As the story goes, a man (representing God in the parable) was preparing a top-notch banquet for valued guests. However, the RSVPs weren't flowing in as the host had expected. Key guests found diverse excuses for refusing the invitation, placing their own limited self-interests over the happiness and offered hospitality of the host. Angered by the refusals to be part of the kingdom party, the man directed his servant to ""'go out quickly into the streets and alleys of the town and bring in the poor, the crippled, the blind and the lame'"" (v. 21). When yet more room remained at the table, the man added, ""'Go out to the roads

and country lanes and compel them to come in, so that my
house will be full. I tell you, not one of those who were invited
will get a taste of my banquet"'"" (vv. 23–24).

I don't know about you, but I don't want to miss out on
what God has offered; I want to join all of my diverse neighbors at the kingdom's banquet. But how often do our own
kitchen or dining room tables model this diversity?

Jesus, of course, didn't just talk about loving neighbors,
he modeled it—to a broad diversity of people. As I noted in
my book *Renegade Gospel: Rebel Jesus*, those to whom Jesus
ministered included "a poor widow with two small coins, a
hemorrhaging woman, lepers, the blind, an unnamed child, an
adulteress, prostitutes, and a short, thieving tax collector who
clambered up a tree to grab a glimpse of Jesus walking by."[19]

While most religious Jews avoided Samaria like the plague,
willingly adding miles and days to a journey in the effort to
steer a wide berth, Jesus passed directly through it. This would
have been a complete anathema to other Jewish rabbis or religious leaders. Worse yet, he chose to identify himself as the
Messiah to a "pagan" Samaritan, a woman who also happened
to have very loose morals (John 4:1–26). What on earth could
Jesus have been thinking? Why was Jesus so "neighborly" with
someone who was completely different from himself?

A Samaritan also played a pivotal role in what is arguably
one of Jesus' most well-known stories, the parable of the Good
Samaritan. In fact, Jesus launched into this parable when an
expert in the Jewish law, hoping to trap Jesus into a theological error, asked a key question that is quite germane to this
chapter: "'And who is my neighbor?'" (Luke 10:29). Instead
of answering directly, Jesus recounted the story of a man who
was beaten and robbed along the road between Jerusalem and
Jericho and left for dead. Two religious leaders passed by the
victim, carefully averting their gaze and denying any responsibility for their beaten Jewish "neighbor." However, a Samaritan traveling the same road stopped, tended to the victim's
wounds, took him to the closest inn for further treatment, and
left behind cash to cover his remaining care.

At the end of the story, Jesus asked the legal expert, "'Which of these three do you think was a neighbor to the man who fell into the hands of robbers?'" The legal expert was forced to reply, "'The one who had mercy on him.'" Jesus directed, "'Go and do likewise.'" I could be wrong, but I don't think Jesus was only talking to the legal expert at that point.

As we noted previously, immigration is a contentious issue. Often those identified as conservative Christians would be considered "hardliners" when it comes to immigration policy, especially when applied to what they would define as "illegal" immigration. Yet the church on the day of Pentecost represented many nations. The Old Testament is filled with declarations as to how God's people were to treat the foreigners among them; that treatment could often be described as downright neighborly. Exodus 22:21 mandates, "Do not mistreat or oppress a foreigner, for you were foreigners in Egypt." Exodus 23:9 sings the same refrain. Leviticus 19:33–34 echoes the theme and adds, "Love them as yourself." Why does that sound so familiar?

The author of Hebrews points out, "Do not forget to show hospitality to strangers, for by so doing some people have shown hospitality to angels without knowing it" (Heb. 13:2). Abraham certainly discovered this in Genesis 18, when God, in the form of three strangers, darkens the doorstep of Abraham's tent. I plan to live out the remainder of my life with a very broad definition of "neighbor"; I don't want to take any chances of missing out on Jesus.

NETWORKED LIVING

I have spent the last several pages proclaiming the importance of inclusive and generous love toward broadly defined neighbors. Yet I live in Tipp City, Ohio, a community that is primarily white and middle class, with a median household income that runs about 15 percent higher than the average for the entire state of Ohio. I have not relocated my home into a neighborhood that is more ethnically and socioeconomically diverse.

In our *Christian Wallet* survey, most respondents also reported living in middle-class or upper-middle-class neighborhoods, and 41 percent estimated that others in the neighborhood had approximately the same income as they. Comparatively few respondents said they live in an economically diverse neighborhood (4 percent) or a neighborhood where "income varies widely" (10 percent). It would be easy for us to bury our heads in the sand and not be aware of our neighbors' plight.

As my friend Shane Claiborne has said, "The great tragedy in the church is not that rich Christians do not care about the poor but that rich Christians do not know the poor. . . . I long for the Calcutta slums to meet the Chicago suburbs, for lepers to meet landowners and for each to see God's image in the other. . . . I truly believe that when the poor meet the rich, riches will have no meaning. And when the rich meet the poor, we will see poverty come to an end."[20]

Shane practices what he preaches, living among the poor in Philadelphia. Because I have not done that, I must be very intentional about building opportunities for practicing love toward wide-ranging neighbors into my life and the life of my church. Our primary campus in Tipp City has always been predominantly white, mirroring the ethnic makeup of the nearest communities. Yet we consider it essential at Ginghamsburg to demonstrate the diversity of the kingdom, so we work to model all types of diversity across our staff, through the folks who lead worship from the stage each weekend and even in the photos of our congregation we choose to include in print and electronic communications.

Our two church restarts are located in very racially and socioeconomically diverse communities. It is important that I visit our Fort McKinley and the Point campuses periodically not just to minister to those parts of our church community but to witness the power and beauty of those multicultural communities. The Point is located in Trotwood, where 66 percent of the population is African American. When my daughter's family lived with Carolyn and me for a number of months during their relocation from Boston to Cincinnati, I signed up to be the assistant coach for a team of four-year-olds in the Trotwood soccer program and enrolled my granddaughter on the team. I don't want her, or myself, to miss out on the beautiful diversity of what it can mean to love our neighbors. It is also why it is essential that every few years I travel to Sudan to visit our projects there and especially the people they are serving. I always come back reenergized and reengaged by the mission and by those I can now more clearly see as my sisters and brothers. I am my brothers' keeper—and they are mine!

I don't agree with all of his editorial viewpoints, but I enjoy reading *New York Times* columnist David Brooks. In a column from July 2014, Brooks opens with the following question: "Is life more like baseball, or is it more like soccer?" Now, anyone who knows me knows that I am baseball obsessed. I am a lifelong Cincinnati Reds fan, and my son was very successful playing college baseball as a catcher for an Ivy League school. Despite my attempt at coaching soccer, I can't say I have ever been much of a fan. As Brooks writes, baseball may be a team sport but it ultimately consists of a bunch of individual activities like hitting or fielding a grounder. He goes on to state, "Most of us spend our days thinking we are playing baseball, but we are really playing soccer," a sport that requires team strategies and team formations to control the ball and to control the space on the field. Brooks notes, "We think we individually choose what career path to take, whom to socialize with, what views to hold. But, in fact, those decisions are shaped by the networks of people around us more than we dare recognize."[21]

I don't want a limited network of only those who look, act, and believe as I do. When that happens, we miss the rich diversity of what God has planned for our lives, our missions, and our ministry. We must find ways to meet our neighbors, all our neighbors, and then love them on purpose.

There are also very personal benefits. A few years ago I

watched a documentary called *Happy*, which shared real life stories of people from around the globe and interviews with scientists researching what happiness is and how we best experience it.[22] One of the stories focused on a single mother with three kids in Denmark, which has consistently ranked as one of the happiest countries on earth. In part Danish happiness has been attributed to its focus on social equality and a high standard of living, but it is perhaps most telling that more Danes live in cohousing communities than is found in any other modern, industrialized country. The documentary posits that we are more likely to find happiness in the context of community. This is certainly true for the Danish family that *Happy* profiled. The mother felt very well supported by the twenty or so families with which they lived. The older residents served as excellent "grandparents" to her children. The rotated meal duty gave her more time after work most evenings to spend time with her children. All families saved money through shared expenses. Her daughter proclaimed that it's "like a big family," and the mother stated, "This place saved me."

At the close of this particular segment, the *Happy* narrator concluded, "When we work together, we realize, 'My life is pretty good as it is and I may have something to give to someone else who does not have what I have.'" I think it boils down to this: God has designed us to live in community; God has designed us to love our neighbors.

As good stewards and good neighbors, we must be prepared to invest the contents of our Christian wallets into meeting our neighbors' needs—especially those on the more unfortunate side of the great socioeconomic divide. But, more significantly, choosing to love our neighbors requires a more difficult investment—our time.

One of Ginghamsburg's other pastors, Jon Morgan, preached recently on the parable of the Good Samaritan, using it to remind us that "there is no such thing as drive-by love." The unpraiseworthy religious leaders in the parable did just that: they drove on by. Hence, no love. The Samaritan, of course, didn't. Love that doesn't walk on by often requires of me two of my most precious things: time and money. The Samaritan gave copious amounts of both. Of those two treasured resources, no matter how cheap you are, the easiest to give is money. In fact, I will step out on a limb here and say that giving money to demonstrate love really *can* be done on a drive-by basis. Toss it in, get that warm flush of feel-goodness, and then keep on running to Jerusalem or Jericho.

But real love takes more than money. It takes time. And that is the treasure we guard most closely of all. We have to get close, deal with the blood, touch the wounds, wrap the bandages, pack up the load, and carry our sister or brother to the next safe place. That kind of love can be tough to give.

Christians are to form a community of light in the midst of darkness. We are not to be a limited community of people who attempt to escape the world but a broad, thriving, and investing community through which God pours heaven's resources and heaven's purposes into planet earth.

QUESTIONS FOR REFLECTION

- What factors did you consider when choosing where to live? Do you feel connected to your neighbors?
- How can you build closer relationships with your physical neighbors, who may be similar to you in lifestyle and values? What about with neighbors who live across town or may be different from you in various ways?

Meet Rusty Eshleman

Rusty Eshleman is in his early thirties, and the father of two: Ella, age four, and Levi, age two. He and his wife Renae have been married for nine years. Rusty serves as the worship and community development pastor for our urban Fort McKinley campus. He and Renae actually bought a home in the Fort

McKinley neighborhood five years ago, a decision that most people would consider risky. As chapter 5 noted, the per capita income of folks who live in Fort McKinley, located on the northwest side of Dayton, is only $18,000. Drug houses, crime, and poverty have been hallmarks of the community. Yet Rusty and Renae are raising their two children there. To understand why, you need to know a little more of their story.

The year before they moved to Fort McKinley, Rusty and Renae spent eleven months with Mission Year (www .missionyear.org) in Atlanta, Georgia, a ministry founded by Tony and Bart Campolo in 1997. Mission Year recruits young Christian adults to spend a year of their lives living and serving in communities in inner-city America. In addition to Atlanta, Mission Year has deployed teams in nine other large cities, including Chicago, Philadelphia, and Houston. Its mission statement is "Love God, Love People, Nothing Else Matters." Mission Year is committed to "placing the needs of our neighbors first and developing committed disciples of Christ with a heart for the poor."

The Mission Year experience, Rusty explained, had three primary purposes. First, it was to teach the team members how to live with one another in community. Perhaps ironically, Rusty and Renae found community living to be the most challenging part of the Mission Year experience. The Eshlemans were housed with two other couples, and Rusty said it was rough. "When we were at home we would frequently find ourselves arguing with the people we lived with. That part of the experience was not awesome, although it did teach us the importance of humility and communication. But our experience in the neighborhood was great!"

The second key focus was for team members to be out in the community, meeting neighbors, building relationships, and serving with local community organizations. Note that the latter was not a paying job. Rusty and Renae had to raise $24,000 for their own support. They didn't work for pay; they paid to work. One of Rusty's jobs was to help fix lunch at Café 458, a unique restaurant staffed by volunteers that serves reservation-only meals to homeless men and women through a fine dining experience. Café 458 wasn't just about a handout, however. Its empowerment ministries included personalized case management to help guests achieve self-sufficiency, access to medical and mental health services, and onsite substance-abuse support groups, among others. Renae's mornings were spent at a large Presbyterian church serving the homeless. The program supplied emergency bags that would include items like granola bars and wet wipes. Perhaps more significantly, the program focused on helping clients acquire or replace lost paperwork needed to receive social services, items like birth certificates, state IDs, and social security cards.

In the afternoons the Eshlemans served with an organization called Raising Expectations, a nonprofit youth development organization focused on tutoring, homework, and after-school programs. Rusty noted, "Education is often the way out of poverty." The kids were also exposed to "enrichment" activities, important to developing new life pictures, including performances, museums, and athletic activities like ice skating.

The third focus for the Mission Year experience was education and discipleship. Mission Year first and foremost wants to develop its team members as Jesus' followers and expose them to new perspectives on a variety of subjects, including interpersonal relationships, social justice, living in multicultural environments, and spiritual growth.

Rusty says one of the greatest lessons from the year in Atlanta was how to serve others humbly and to honor the innate dignity that every single individual has, regardless of where he or she lives. "Everyone has something to offer; I can't judge others by what I consider 'normal.' My normal is only descriptive of me; not prescriptive for others. Spiritually, I discovered that I hadn't come to Atlanta to bring Jesus but to find Jesus. We needed to learn that we are not 'bringing' light into dark places. There is prevenient grace. Jesus is always working in front of us, not behind us." Rusty concluded, "Many people thought I went on Mission Year to save people, but I am the one who got 'saved.'"

When Mission Year ended, Rusty and Renae knew they had been ruined in terms of following what many know as the conventional path to a typical home in the suburbs. Unemployed, they moved back to this region to be close to Renae's family and started looking for God's next call. A relative invited them to visit our Fort McKinley campus. Rusty was about to take a job as a restaurant manager, when the Fort McKinley worship leader position was posted. And so the next chapter for the Eshlemans began. Committed to being a neighborhood pastor in a neighborhood church, Rusty and Renae purchased their current home in this most challenging of neighborhoods. I asked Rusty about the difficulties they encounter. "It can be a little bit crazy in our neighborhood. Some neighbors live pretty chaotic lives, and our kids are being exposed to that. Family relationships are not strong. There are drugs in the neighborhood; one of our neighbors is selling. Establishing friendships is tough. For one thing, we schedule stuff; many of our neighbors live in the moment."

The Eshlemans have developed a few significant relationships. An older couple "adopted" them as if they were grandkids, and Rusty and Renae were able to house and care for the wife temporarily after the loss of her husband. Even now this widow occasionally dog-sits and folds laundry for the Eshleman family, and they help her with yard work. Rusty and Renae have also been trying to model what a healthy married relationship looks like to a young couple in the neighborhood who invited the Eshlemans to witness their courthouse wedding. "Healthy marriage," Rusty wryly noted, "is not a life picture they currently have."

"Mostly" Rusty said, "we just try to be present in and to the neighborhood. We take the dog and kids for a walk, stop and chat, push a doublewide stroller—in a sense we appear to be living a very middle-class life in a non-middle-class neighborhood. But, the people have seen us stay; we have not left. We sometimes help our neighbors with stuff like fixing a mailbox; they sometimes help us. We are not here to be the saviors of the neighborhood; we are here to be authentic; we are here to be neighbors."

I asked Rusty if they were tempted to leave. "Even if tomorrow Ginghamsburg Church told us, 'We can't pay you anymore,' I am not moving. We feel called to the Fort McKinley neighborhood."

10

The Joy of Simplicity

Amazon.com, the distributor of pretty much any item a person could want to purchase, offers more than 66,000 products related to the search term "simple living." I had to smile thinking how buying, reading, and storing the 19,848 books included in that list might represent the very antithesis of living a simpler lifestyle. Clearly, this is a tremendous felt need in our culture. So why are we so bad at it?

Despite this seemingly deep desire to downsize, simplify, and relax, we still wear two things as our primary badges of honor and self-worth—our stuff and our busyness. My house is bigger, my car is sportier, and my phone is thinner than yours. My "vacation" was more elaborate. I was away from home five nights this week for church business; you can only claim two. Therefore I must be more popular *and* important—not to mention exhausted. Our penchant for bigger, better, and more both in our possessions and our calendars simply isn't healthy or sustainable.

Carolyn Gregoire's article "The Psychology of Materialism: Why It's Making You Unhappy," recently highlighted that, according to the American Psychological Association,

Americans' rate of well-being has declined since the 1950s while consumption has increased. Gregoire also points out that materialistic values are linked to type A behaviors like aggression and competitiveness; a focus on materialism is frequently linked to unhappiness in marriages; and our consumer culture may contribute to developing narcissistic personalities and behaviors. She quotes psychologist Tim Kasser, who states, "Narcissists generally act with arrogance and are deeply concerned with issues of personal adequacy, seeking power and prestige to cover for feelings of inner emptiness and low self-worth."[1]

Ironically perhaps, a study published in the *Journal of Consumer Research* found a relationship between materialism and loneliness. Materialism tends to foster social isolation, and social isolation in return fosters materialism, or attachment to our possessions versus attachments to people.[2]

Our overly packed schedules aren't doing us any favors either. According to an article in *The Economist*, our busyness may be more of a perception problem than a reality. On average people in wealthier companies have more nonworking time now than they used to have. As the author noted, "Ever since a clock was first used to synchronize labor in the 18th century, time has been understood in relation to money. Once hours are financially quantified, people worry more about wasting, saving or using them profitably. When economies grow and incomes rise, everyone's time becomes more valuable. And the more valuable something becomes, the scarcer it seems."[3]

This "time is money" mind-set creates an urgency to make every moment count. So we pack our schedules and feel guilty when we set aside time for leisure or even key relationships. The article also shared that the explosion of available goods has contributed to our time and schedule stress. Choosing what to eat, watch, and wear across so many available options contributes to feelings of stress. As the author stated, "The endless possibilities afforded by a simple internet connection boggle the mind"—exactly my experience when I received Amazon hits on 66,000-plus "simple living" products. Our access to too many choices also tempts us to spend more than we can afford, increasing our stress to unsustainable levels.

KEEPING MARGINS IN LIFE

Think of a piece of notebook paper—or the pages of this very book. The writing does not fill every inch of the paper but leaves a margin around the edges, making the text easier and more enjoyable to read. We need margins in life too. The concept of maintaining a Sabbath, or a margin of time in our week, is stressed throughout Scripture. We first see it in the book of Genesis, as God models it. At the close of the six-day creation story, we read in Genesis 2:2, "By the seventh day God had finished the work he had been doing; so on the seventh day he rested from all his work. Then God blessed the seventh day and made it holy, because on it he rested from all the work of creating that he had done." By the second book of the Bible, we see God commanding the Sabbath as part of the Ten Commandments in Exodus 20:8–10: "'Remember the Sabbath day by keeping it holy. Six days you shall labor and do all your work, but the seventh day is a sabbath to the LORD your God. On it you shall not do any work, neither you, nor your son or daughter, nor your male or female servant, nor your animals, nor any foreigner residing in your towns.'"

The word *Sabbath* appears 154 times throughout Scripture in the NIV. Yet Jesus also clarified that the Sabbath was not simply some arbitrary, legalistic practice that God dictated, pointing out in Mark 2:27 that "the Sabbath was made for [people], not [people] for the Sabbath." God knows that we need Sabbath rhythms in our relationships, in our economic practices, and in all the dimensions of our lives. God has the well-being of his children in mind.

To illustrate, let's look again at Isaiah 5:8: "Woe to you who add house to house and join field to field till no space is left and you live alone in the land." Isaiah is talking about relational margins. When we keep chasing a lifestyle that is about

bigger, better, and more, we too have no space left for significant relationships. We are left to "live alone in the land." God
is a God of relationships. God created us for relationship with
God but also for right relationship with one another. These
are intertwined. For instance, it's difficult for me to be in right
relationship with God unless I am also in right relationship
with my wife, Carolyn.

When we chase stuff, when we are chasing the so-called
American dream, we leave no time or margins for relationships. We harm some of the people we claim to care about the
most by ignoring them; we simply don't have time for spouses,
children, parents, or friends as we work more hours to buy
more stuff and then spend our time at home taking care of
it all. Or we oppress others to ensure our own materialistic
desires are met. As we read earlier in Isaiah 58, the people of
Judah cried out to God, wondering why they were seeing no
fruit from their diligent religious practices. God responded via
Isaiah, "'Yet on the day of your fasting, you do as you please
and exploit all your workers. Your fasting ends in quarreling
and strife, and in striking each other with wicked fists'" (Isa.
58:3–4). Jesus himself both modeled and repeated the need for
right relationship with God and others throughout his ministry, going so far as to say in Matthew 5:23–24: "'Therefore, if
you are offering your gift at the altar and there remember that
your brother or sister has something against you, leave your gift
there in front of the altar. First go and be reconciled to them;
then come and offer your gift.'"

We form and grow relationships in the margins of our lives.
It is also within those margins that we do acts of kindness or service toward others. Most critically, it is in the margins that we
build our right relationship with God. This is why I am in my
study by 5:30 a.m. every morning; I am working on that most
critical relationship. We also need to be cognizant of how our
no-margin-lifestyle decisions are impacting our children. What
priorities are we modeling? I had a young parent admit to me
the other day that he skips pages in bedtime books whenever
he can get away with it just because he is so exhausted. I highly

doubt he's the only one. I love my grandchildren beyond distraction, but when they spend the night with me and Carolyn even I am tempted to try bedtime shortcuts just to get back more quickly to whatever else I think I need to be doing.

The only things that live beyond us or that we can take with us are the investments we have made in relationships. Yet we constantly sacrifice them on the altar of too much stuff and overstuffed schedules. We add "house to house" and eventually find ourselves "alone in the land."

Even when we are in the same room as our loved ones, just "relaxing," we fill that margin of time with media at the cost of face-to-face connection. On average, U.S. adults spend over forty minutes per day on Facebook. Tumblr places second with thirty-four minutes, followed by Instagram, Pinterest, Twitter, and Snapchat.[4] God help those of us who use all of those platforms. I was seated at a table in a restaurant the other evening next to a family of four I did not know. I never caught one of them glancing up from his or her smartphone long enough to have a conversation.

Similarly, we turn mealtime—what could and should be a margin in our day to reenergize and reconnect with others—into another "to do" to be checked off the list as efficiently as possible. DoSomething.org reported that one in four Americans eat fast food every day and spend up to 10 percent of their disposable income on fast food each year.[5] We aren't gathering around the family table very often for leisurely meals and conversation. In 2015, for the first time since the U.S. Census Bureau started tracking in 1992, Americans are spending more money in restaurants and bars than we are in grocery stores, affecting not just our margins for home and family but our economic margins as well.[6]

As we noted in chapter 4, God expects us to live within economic margins, not eating everything we produce by ourselves. Deuteronomy 24 directed in three verses that we are not to harvest to the very edges of our fields but to leave some behind for the poor, needy, and disenfranchised. Those of us who have opportunities and incomes are to use them in part to bless others. With great blessing comes great responsibility. We are God's means of provision. As Richard Foster asked in *Freedom of Simplicity*, "Can God be pleased by the vast and increasing inequities among us? Is he not grieved by our arrogant accumulation, while Christian brothers and sisters elsewhere languish and die? . . . Is there not an obligation upon us to do justice, and to love mercy, and to walk humbly with God if we want to live in his wonderful peace?"[7]

Sadly, many of us not only fail to maintain margins within our means but go actively into debt to acquire bigger, better, and more. Anytime we go into debt, we are spending beyond the edges of our own harvest. It doesn't matter if we can afford the monthly payment. Whenever we are in debt, we will be working into the future to pay for the past. That is clearly not God's design.

TRUE SIMPLICITY

I sometimes watch the HGTV show *House Hunters*, in which a real estate agent shows prospective buyers three homes available for purchase that meet the buyers' stated preferences for features, location, and price range.[8] Inevitably, however, it seems like the realtor manages to work in for the first or second visit a home that is absolutely gorgeous but priced higher than the buyers' budget. The subsequent homes toured just can't quite seem to measure up. Too many times, the buyers succumb to temptation and buy the biggest and best, taking on extra debt and extra pressure to maintain more house than they really need. Gotcha! It's time for us to right-size our lifestyles.

Materialism—this desire for bigger, more, or better—is a spirit-killing addiction. Foster says, "All of us feel that we are in complete control of our desire for things. We would never admit to an ungovernable spirit of covetousness. The problem is that we, like the alcoholic, are unable to recognize the disease once we have been engulfed by it."[9]

How do we break free from this addiction and live more simply? As he does in so many ways, Christ provides us with the ultimate example. As Foster says,

> Jesus Christ and all the writers of the New Testament call us to break free of mammon lust and live in joyous trust. . . . They point us toward a way of living in which everything we have we receive as a gift, and everything we have is cared for by God, and everything we have is available to others when it is right and good. This reality frames the heart of Christian simplicity.[10]

Jesus himself lived in such a way that he was unencumbered for the mission, and he taught the disciples to do the same. When a teacher of the law approached Jesus indicating that he wanted to become a disciple, Jesus replied, "'Foxes have dens and birds have nests, but the Son of Man has no place to lay his head'" (Matt. 8:20).

When Jesus sent out his disciples on their initial independent forays to propel the mission forward without Jesus at their side, he instructed them to "'take nothing for the journey—no staff, no bag, no bread, no money, no extra shirt. Whatever house you enter, stay there until you leave that town'" (Luke 9:3–4). Again in Luke 10:4 the instructions were "'Do not take a purse or bag or sandals.'" These instructions no doubt accomplished two things: they allowed the disciples to serve proactively unhampered by stuff and taught them to rely on God's provision.

The apostle Paul too seemed to have a very itinerant lifestyle after his conversion, with friends, church leaders, and often jailers as his housing hosts and working as a tent maker (or building subcontractor) as needed to make a little income. Paul clearly did not miss the "stuff," declaring in Philippians 4:11–13, "I have learned to be content whatever the circumstances. I know what it is to be in need, and I know what it is to have plenty. I have learned the secret of being content in any and every situation, whether well fed or hungry, whether living in plenty or in want. I can do all this through him who gives me strength."

I also don't believe that God designed all of us to be itinerant or to surrender completely our earthly goods. It is much more about how we prioritize the use of the resources with which we have been entrusted. Are we investing in kingdom purposes, in that which will live beyond us? Bill and Melinda Gates, founders of the Bill and Melinda Gates Foundation, are Roman Catholics. The foundation is the largest private foundation in the world and is focused globally on health care, reduction of extreme poverty, and expansion of educational opportunities. Their wealth is being deployed carefully and thoughtfully over years to accomplish good. That would not be the case had they simply surrendered it all in bulk or on a whim. I have no interest in "rich bashing," just in the wise stewardship of our means and gifts.

In *The Companion Bible*, E. W. Bullinger comments on Matthew 19:24, the oft-quoted verse when Jesus said to his disciples, "'It is easier for a camel to go through the eye of a needle than for someone who is rich to enter the kingdom of God.'" Many presume that Jesus is referring to a sewing needle, but Bullinger believes that the eye of the needle Jesus was referencing was a small door that typically existed as part of a larger gate, which was the only way to enter certain cities after dark. A wealthy merchant on a camel carrying his packs could never fit; the camel first had to be unloaded of the merchant's goods and wealth. If we are unwilling to unload our possessions, we may find it difficult to enter the narrow gate (see Matt. 7:13).[11]

We've all heard the saying "You can't take it with you." In Isaiah 5:9 the prophet says this very thing: "The LORD Almighty has declared in my hearing: 'Surely the great houses will become desolate, the fine mansions left without occupants.'" We invest so much of our two primary resources—time and money—into great houses and fine mansions, yet we can't take it with us. If you have ever had a parent die or downsize, you may know what I mean. What were once considered treasures are now inconveniences that must be sorted, stored, or discarded. I did, however, find a few lasting treasures when I went through my dad's drawers in a rolltop desk after he passed away. They included cards that my sister and I had made for him out of paper and crayons saying, "I love you, Daddy." I also found a clay ashtray that I had once made for him in Boy Scouts. But note that these "treasures" were all somehow tied to those key relationships in his life. When we don't pay attention to the relationships, we are forgetting that the "houses will become desolate, the fine mansions left without occupants." I recently heard the story of a man who had spent forty years of his life collecting an impressive array of antiques; they all sold within an hour at an auction after he died. Where and how are we investing our resources?

Even in secular America, we are beginning to see more of a trend toward choosing a simpler lifestyle. One popular example is the "small-house movement" as evidenced in the cable TV show *Tiny House Nation*.[12] A *Huffington Post* infograph published in late 2014 indicated that the average size of new houses rose from 1,525 square feet in 1973 to 2,598 square feet in 2013.[13] That trend now appears to be reversing. It's hard to track down accurate statistics in the United States since the small-house sizes do not require the same building permits as a larger home. But it is suspected to be growing in popular culture. The article goes on to note the plusses for jumping on the tiny-home bandwagon, including a reduced carbon footprint, lower taxes, less maintenance or debt, and the reduced price to purchase or build. Chore time invested in the cleaning and upkeep of the home is also minimized. Plus you accumulate less stuff because there is simply not room for it.

A number of popular bloggers are living the minimalist lifestyle and eagerly share their findings with others. Kathy Gottberg, a blogger for the *Huffington Post*, gave her and her husband Thom's top-ten commandments for simple living. Many of them echo biblical themes although hers is not a faith-based viewpoint per se. One commandment is to remember that less is more. As Gottberg puts it, "'More-ness' only complicates, confuses, and distracts us from the peace, joy, and freedom that a minimal life offers." She also notes that debt is the worst poverty and that we should treasure our relationships, not our possessions. Sound familiar? She concludes, "Life is short—do what matters."[14]

U.S. News & World Report claims that simple living leads to improved health. An unpublished University of the Sciences in Pennsylvania study found that "90 percent of people who identified as part of the simple living movement reported improved physical health after voluntarily making a change to earn less money."[15]

It's not just the middle class who may choose to pursue a simpler lifestyle. I recently received a newsletter from one of the financial groups with which I invest with an article titled "The Frugal Habits of Millionaires."[16] It profiled Warren Buffett, the well-known billionaire who still lives in a modest home in Omaha, Nebraska, that he bought for $31,500 in 1958, and indicated that Facebook billionaire Mark Zuckerberg drives an Acura TSX, an "entry-level luxury car," and that the top car brand among millionaires is Toyota, not a BMW or Mercedes as one might suspect. I will never experience the amount of wealth that Zuckerberg and Buffett have accumulated, but they too must clearly see that abundant life is not found solely on the basis of our toys, possessions, or pocketbooks.

CHRISTIAN WALLET PRINCIPLES

So, as Christians, how are we to view our money? I hope you've noticed some trends emerge as we've explored the various aspects of how we are to view and use our Christian wallets. My research, prayer, and discernment regarding my own "wallet" has led me to a number of key conclusions:

- All of my wallet's contents, every single penny, come from God. I am the steward, not the owner.
- My wallet is one crucial form of God's provision within my life. It enables me to take care of my family and myself and to serve others. My intent for deploying its

contents is to be focused on others, not on myself. I am responsible for asking myself daily, "How can I live more simply so that others can simply live?"

- Gratitude is critical. I will never enjoy what I already have, and God will not trust me with more if I fail to have an attitude of gratitude.

- My wallet's contents are an investment tool for God's kingdom purposes, not intended for self-centered hoarding. I either trust God for my daily provision, my daily bread, or I don't. I must release it before God will increase it.

- Earthly treasure is temporal, not eternal. I cannot take it with me and suspect I won't even want to when I reach the end of my life. My Christian wallet is to focus on that which will outlast my physical presence on planet earth. Jesus said it better: "'Do not store up for yourselves treasures on earth, where moths and vermin destroy, and where thieves break in and steal. But store up for yourselves treasures in heaven, where moths and vermin do not destroy, and where thieves do not break in and steal. For where your treasure is, there your heart will be also'" (Matt. 6:19–21).

- My wallet is to be used to accomplish God's good, never to propagate evil, including the exploitation of other people or reckless, unthinking destruction of the earth's resources.

- Money is not something I should spend every waking moment thinking or worrying about. Money in and of itself is not evil; it is simply provision. But as the apostle Paul said in 1 Timothy 6:10, the *love* of money could get me into all kinds of trouble.

- Money will never bring me contentment—no matter how much or how little I have. Contentment is found in relationship with Christ and with one another.

Ultimately, we each make a choice, consciously or unconsciously, to invest our God-provided resources in serving ourselves or serving God's purposes. The first is selfish and short-sighted; the latter leads to new hope and renewed life. From this point forward with my own Christian wallet, I choose life.

QUESTIONS FOR REFLECTION

- What areas of your life need wider margins? Do you need to simplify your schedule, spending, or belongings?
- What changes do you need to make to live a lifestyle and manage a wallet that are more in keeping with God's values and vision?

Meet Kim Miller

Kim Miller is possibly the most creative person I have ever encountered, and in her twenty years of ministry at Ginghamsburg Church she has been instrumental to its mission. She first joined the staff team as an unpaid servant who offered to help with children's choir. Soon, Kim was my weekly partner in creating our worship-design-team process, serving as the creative director for each weekend's worship. She now uses her talents to enhance all of our campus spaces, whether it be a room remodel, a stage design for a specific message series, or a special lobby display for a Mother's Day flower sale.

Kim has also been instrumental in creating Ginghamsburg's "mud and spit" theology. Why buy when you can repurpose? Why not explore and use what's already in your hand? Her eye for reclaiming and redeploying combined with creativity and elbow grease have allowed Kim, her husband, Clark, and her loyal team of unpaid servants to create beautiful and inspiring worship stage designs, often for less than a hundred bucks. I have literally watched Kim convert trash into treasure. Once she and I were part of a small workshop being held in our youth building, not the most welcoming of spaces. Dismayed to find no décor in the workshop room, Kim emerged a few moments later from the building's kitchen with a candle and stiff brown paper towel. After artfully crumpling the paper towel, she placed it in the center of the small table we were to gather around, added the candle on top, and then lit it. Voila! A table centerpiece. If I had done that, it would have looked like a crumpled brown paper towel, trash that was ready to be discarded. In Kim's hands it became art. I think one of the attendees wanted to take it home following the workshop.

Kim has been married to Clark for thirty-nine years, marrying young at ages nineteen and twenty-one, respectively. Their family now includes three married children with spouses and eight grandchildren. Kim and Clark have an incredibly strong marriage based on shared values. Kim explained, "We have been do-it-yourselfers from the very beginning. That was one of the things that attracted me to Clark. While we may not have always been able to buy everything we may have thought we wanted, at least that which was worth having we have been able to make." Clark and Kim also have lived simply, not adjusting their lifestyle regardless of income. The Millers are also debt free. Kim noted, "Money has never been our primary currency; we operate instead in time, skills, energy, and dreams. Our intent is always to live so that we can, at a moment's notice, be available for wherever God's call may take us."

Kim is a wise steward of the earth's resources. She was taking her own reusable bags to do her grocery shopping long before it became trendy. She and Clark keep a compost pile in their postage-stamp-sized backyard. They are thrifty—and healthy—in their food choices, striving to waste as little as possible. Kim is always cognizant that "the trash truck may haul it off, but that does not mean it goes away." Kim added, "For some reason, that thought makes my head hurt. My bywords are repurpose, restore, and recycle." When I asked Kim why she cares so much, she responded, "All I know is that someday I will stand before God. I have the stewardship of this one life. I will max it out with however much influence I may have to model kingdom purposes."

Kim clearly finds joy in simplicity. When I asked her about that, she said, "More toys means less joy each toy receives. When we continue to accumulate stuff, our joy becomes so diluted that we can no longer find it anymore. It becomes meaningless." When I asked her what she loves the most, she quickly responded, "I love, love, love being in my home. I love the simplicity of making a meal and sitting down and sharing it with others. It just doesn't get any better."

In addition, Kim noted the freedom that she and Clark feel within their chosen lifestyle. "If you were a bystander at our kitchen table as we debrief at the end of the day, you would never hear us talking about how we will pay our bills. We don't talk about money; we talk about dreams. Money isn't our god; God is our God. We are grateful, and we are ready to go. Money will never be the barrier."

I enjoy being Facebook friends with Kim because you are able to gain a small glimpse of how she deploys her creative, repurposing gifts in her personal life. Recently, she posted a picture of her twenty-year-old refrigerator, freshly decoupaged for a brand new look. Another time she posted a picture of herself in a sweater that she had "Kim-ized." She had spotted it in another Facebook friend's post in a pile of clothing to be donated to Goodwill. In Kim's hands, it was newly gorgeous. Kim recently decorated her home beautifully with twigs and branches from her neighbors' cuttings. "I just needed to grab them before the trash truck arrived," she said.

Kim roots her drive to live simply—and creatively—in her somewhat difficult childhood. "My dad had very fine taste but was the cause of dysfunction within the family." Although Kim's family lived in a nice neighborhood, family finances were tight with any disposable income supporting her father's beer and cigarette habits. By the eighth grade, Kim's parents had divorced, leaving her mom as a single mother of five children, struggling to make ends meet. When Kim was in high school, her boyfriend's family invited Kim to accompany them on vacation to a luxury resort in Georgia. Kim said, "I fell in love with what that lifestyle represented. I loved the 'beautiful things' that it demonstrated. I knew when I went back home that I would not be able to acquire that kind of beauty, but I could create it into existence. Eventually I realized that the kingdom of God provides the complete picture of ultimate beauty; I am God's co-creator to bring that beauty into existence."

Epilogue

One of the books that I read in preparation for this project was *FREE: Spending Your Time and Money on What Matters Most*, by Mark and Lisa Scandrette. As I taught on the Christian wallet to my own Ginghamsburg Church family, I reflected daily on the Scandrette's "Prayer of Abundance." I invite you to pray this prayer with me as we commit together from this moment forward to save, spend, give, and live with a conscience.

I know that I am cared for by an Abundant Provider.
I choose to be grateful and trusting.
I believe I have enough and that what I need
    will always be provided.
I choose to be content and generous.
I know that my choices matter for myself, for others
    and for future generations.
Help me to live consciously and creatively, celebrating signs
    of your new creation that is present and coming.
Creator, who made me to seek the greater good of your
        kingdom,

Guide me to use my time, talents and resources
    to pursue what matters most.
Teach me to be free,
    to live without worry, fear or greed in the freedom of
        your abundance.
Give me my daily bread, as I share with those in need.
Thank you for this precious gift of life![1]

Amen and amen.

Notes

Introduction

1. John Kavanagh, *Following Christ in a Consumer Society* (Maryknoll, NY: Orbis Books, 2006), 61, 63.

2. Jen Hatmaker, *7: An Experimental Mutiny against Excess* (Nashville: B&H Publishing Group, 2012), 70.

3. Ibid., 66.

Chapter 1: Culture of Consumerism

1. "Experience the New Buick Enclave," YouTube video, https://www.youtube.com/watch?v=3PINPZr6loY.

2. Donald W. Black, "A Review of Compulsive Buying Disorder," *World Psychiatry* 6, no. 1 (2007): 14–18, http://www.ncbi.nlm.nih.gov/pmc/articles/PMC1805733/.

3. *Urban Cowboy*, soundtrack, Elektra, 1980, compact disc.

4. Bootie Cosgrove-Mather, "Americans Have Negative Savings Rate," *CBS News*, February 7, 2006, http://www.cbsnews.com/news/americans-have-negative-savings-rate/.

5. Allison Schrager, "Consumer Debt Hits an All-Time High" *Bloomberg Business*, September 30, 2014, http://www.businessweek.com/articles/2014-09-30/consumer-debt-hits-an-all-time-high.

6. Quentin Fottrell, "American Credit-Card Debt Hits a Post-Recession High," *Market Watch*, September 13, 2014, http://www.marketwatch.com/story/american-credit-card-debt-hits-new-highs-2014-09-11.

7. Mary Hiers, "What Is the Average American Credit Card Balance?" *Mintlife* (blog), April 9, 2014, https://www.mint.com/blog/credit/what-is-the-average-american-credit-card-balance-0414/.

8. "Global Launch of 2014 Human Development Report," United Nations Development Program, 2014, http://hdr.undp.org/en/2014-report.

9. Winnie Byanyima, "Richest 1% Will Own More than All the Rest by 2016" (press release, Oxfam International, January 19, 2015), https://www

.oxfam.org/en/pressroom/pressreleases/2015-01-19/richest-1-will-own-more-all-rest-2016.

10. Mark Rice-Oxley, "Pope Francis: The Humble Pontiff with Practical Approach to Poverty," March 13, 2013, http://www.theguardian.com/world/2013/mar/13/jorge-mario-bergoglio-pope-poverty.

11. Kathy Grannis Allen, "Gift Givers Plan to Splurge on Friends, Family This Holiday Season" (press release, October 16, 2014), https://nrf.com/media/press-releases/gift-givers-plan-splurge-friends-family-this-holiday-season.

12. "Adult Obesity Facts," Centers for Disease Control & Prevention, June 16, 2015, http://www.cdc.gov/obesity/data/adult.html.

13. "The State of Consumption Today," World Watch Institute, 2013, http://www.worldwatch.org/node/810.

14. "Total Petroleum and Other Liquids Production—2014," U.S. Energy Information Administration (EIA), accessed January 10, 2015, http://www.eia.gov/countries/index.cfm?topL=con.

15. According to Census.gov's current estimate of 2015 population by country, China has almost 1.4 billion people compared to the United States's 321 million people; www.census.gov/population/international/data/countryrank/rank.php., accessed May 1, 2015.

16. "Total Petroleum Consumption–2013," U.S. Energy Information Administration (EIA), accessed January 10, 2015, http://www.eia.gov/countries/index.cfm?view=consumption.

17. "Global Greenhouse Gas Emissions Data," United States Environmental Protection Agency, July 21, 2015, http://www.epa.gov/climatechange/ghgemissions/global.html.

18. "Municipal Solid Waste Generation, Recycling, and Disposal in the United States: Facts and Figures for 2012," United States Environmental Protection Agency, 2012, http://www.epa.gov/epawaste/nonhaz/municipal/pubs/2012_msw_fs.pdf.

19. Graeme Wood, "The Secrets of the Super-rich," *Atlantic*, April 2011, http://www.theatlantic.com/magazine/print/2011/04/secret-fears-of-the-super-rich/308419/.

Chapter 2: Balancing the Budget

1. Dennis Jacobe, "One in Three Americans Prepare a Detailed Household Budget–Thirty Percent Prepare a Long-Term Financial Plan with Investment," Gallup, June 3, 2013, http://www.gallup.com/poll/162872/one-three-americans-prepare-detailed-household-budget.aspx?version=print.

2. "Consumer Expenditures (Annual) News Release,"(press release, U.S. Bureau of Labor Statistics, September 9, 2014), http://data.bls.gov/cgi-bin/print.pl/news.release/archives/cesan_09092014.htm.

3. Mike Holmes, "What Would Happen if the Church Tithed," *Relevant*

Magazine, July 10, 2013, http://www.relevantmagazine.com/god/church/
what-would-happen-if-church-tithed.

4. Jacobe, "One in Three Americans Prepare a Detailed Household,"
http://www.gallup.com/poll/162872/one-three-americans-prepare-detailed-
household-budget.aspx?version=print.

5. Bruce Horovitz, "Halloween Costumes Go to the Dogs These Days,"
USA Today, September 25, 2012, http://usatoday30.usatoday.com/money/
business/story/2012/09/25/halloween-dogs/57842278/1.

6. David Pogue, "A Baffling Phenomenon: Customized Ringtones,"
New York Times (blog), September 13, 2007, http://pogue.blogs.nytimes
.com/2007/09/13/a-baffling-new-phenomenon-customized-ringtones/?_r=0.

7. Katherine Muniz, the Motley Fool, "20 Ways Americans Are Blowing
Their Money," March 24, 2014, http://www.usatoday.com/story/money/
personalfinance/2014/03/24/20-ways-we-blow-our-money/6826633/.

8. "The Toddler's Creed Poem & Rules of Possession," Famlii (blog),
accessed January 17, 2015, http://www.famlii.com/toddler-rules-of-possession-
toddlers-creed/.

9. Mary Hiers, "What Is the Average American Credit Card Balance?"
Mintlife (blog), April 9, 2014, https://www.mint.com/blog/credit/what-is-the-
average-american-credit-card-balance-0414/

10. Dan E. Krane, "Responsibility for Student Debt Must Be Shared,"
Dayton Daily News, October 2, 2014.

11. "529 Plans: Questions and Answers," IRS, September 23, 2014, http://
www.irs.gov/uac/529-Plans:-Questions-and-Answers.

Chapter 3: Conscious Spending

1. Liz Szabo, "Diabetes Rates Skyrocket in Kids and Teens," *USA Today,*
May 3, 2014, http://www.usatoday.com/story/news/nation/2014/05/03/
diabetes-rises-in-kids/8604213/.

2. "Food Availability (per Capita) Data System: Summary Findings,"
USDA, July 22, 2015, http://www.ers.usda.gov/data-products/food-
availability-(per-capita)-data-system/summary-findings.aspx.

3. Jean C. Buzby, Hodan F. Wells, and Jeffrey Hyman, "Calories of Post
Harvest Food Losses at the Retail and Consumer Levels in the United States,"
United States Department of Agriculture, February 2014, http://www.ers.
usda.gov/media/1282296/eib121.pdf.

4. Ibid., 2.

5. Ibid., 7.

6. "Global Launch of 2014 Human Development Report," United Nations
Development Program, 2014, http://hdr.undp.org/en/2014-report.

7. Jeffrey Kugler, "Troubled Waters," *Time,* February 2, 2015, 16, http://
time.com/3678078/troubled-waters.

8. Brian Halweil, "Good Stuff?" Worldwatch Institute, 2004, http://www .worldwatch.org/system/files/GoodStuffGuide_0.pdf.

9. "ILO 2012 Global Estimate of Forced Labour Executive Summary," International Labour Organization, accessed January 24, 2015, http:// www.ilo.org/wcmsp5/groups/public/@ed_norm/@declaration/documents/ publication/wcms_181953.pdf.

10. "Resources for Speakers on Global Issues: Child Labour," United Nations, accessed January 24, 2015, http://www.un.org/en/globalissues/ briefingpapers/childlabour/vitalstats.shtml.

11. "Occupational Safety and Health in the Supply Chain," United Nations Global Compact, accessed January 17, 2015, https://www.unglobalcompact. org/docs/issues_doc/labour/tools_guidance_materials/Occupational_Safety_ Health_in_the_Supply_Chain.pdf.

12. Elizabeth W. Collier and Charles R. Strain, eds. *Religious and Ethical Perspectives on Global Migration* (Lanham, MD: Lexington Books, 2014), 298.

13. "2014 Trafficking in Persons Report," U.S. Department of State, June 20, 2014, http://m.state.gov/md226844.htm.

14. "Death Toll in Philippines Slipper Factory Fire Rises to 72," *Fox News*, May 14, 2015, http://www.foxnews.com/world/2015/05/14/philippines-slipper-factory-fire/.

15. "Building Collapse in Bangladesh Leaves Scores Dead," *New York Times*, April 24, 2013, http://www.nytimes.com/2013/04/25/world/asia/bangladesh -building-collapse.html?pagewanted=all.

16. Ibid.

17. Brenna McGowan, "Disney: Where Dreams Come True?" IHS Child Slave Labor (blog), January 2014, http://ihscslnews.org/view_article .php?id=391.

18. Baratunde Thurston, "Hopping Off the New-Device Treadmill." *Fast Company*, no. 192, February 2015, 104, http://www.fastcompany .com/3039892/one-more-thing/hopping-off-the-new-device-treadmill.

19. Allie Bidwell, "U.N. Seeks to Solve Growing Global E-Waste Problem," *U.S. News*, December 16, 2013, http://www.usnews.com/news/ articles/2013/12/16/un-seeks-to-solve-growing-global-e-waste-problem.

20. "Retail Attraction and Market Research," Andersonville Chamber of Commerce, 2014, http://www.andersonville.org/business-resources/retail-attraction-market-research/.

21. Judith D. Schwartz, "Buying Local: How It Boosts the Economy," *Time*, June 11, 2009, http://content.time.com/time/business/ article/0,8599,1903632,00.html.

22. Robert Safian, "Find Your Mission," *Fast Company*, no. 190, November 2014, 68, 70, http://www.fastcompany.com/3035975/generation-flux/find-your-mission.

23. Danielle Sacks, "Patagonia CEO Rose Marcario Fights the Fights Worth Fighting," *Fast Company*, no. 192, February 2015, 36, http://www

.fastcompany.com/3039739/creative-conversations/patagonia-ceo-rose-marcario-fights-the-fights-worth-fighting.

24. L.N. Smith, *Sunrise over Disney* (Madison, WI: L. N. Smith Publishing, 2011), 428.

Chapter 4: Generosity

1. "Bono Vox (U2)–Interview 7/9," YouTube video, 5:42, posted by maniauswien, March 27, 2008, https://www.youtube.com/watch?v=7JVYbrF93bw..

2. "Consumer Expenditures (Annual) News Release," U.S. Bureau of Labor Statistics, September 9, 2014, http://data.bls.gov/cgibin/print.pl/news.release/archives/cesan_09092014.htm.

3. I was not surprised to see the results of our *Christian Wallet* survey show that 56 percent of respondents report giving away more than 10 percent of their income, given that the majority of respondents are part of the Ginghamsburg Church community. As you might guess from this chapter, the biblical tithe and abundant generosity are topics of great emphasis at Ginghamsburg.

4. Mark Hrywna, "Giving Estimated at $335.17 Billion for 2013," *NonProfit Times*, June 17, 2014, http://www.thenonprofittimes.com/news-articles/giving-usa-2013/.

5. Mike Holmes, "What Would Happen if the Church Tithed?," *Relevant Magazine*, July 10, 2013, http://www.relevantmagazine.com/god/church/what-would-happen-if-church-tithed.

6. "10 Million Tithers Donate More than $50 Billion," *Christianity Today*, 2013, http://www.christianitytoday.org/mediaroom/news/2013/10-million-tithers-donate-more-than-50-billion.html.

7. Ibid.

8. Mike Slaughter, *Upside Living in a Downside Economy* (Nashville: Abingdon Press, 2009).

9. Karen Swallow Prior, "Why Are Christians Such Bad Tippers," *Christianity Today*, January 2013, http://www.christianitytoday.com/women/2013/january/why-are-christians-such-bad-tippers.html

10. BruinKid, "MUST-SEE: Bill Maher BLASTS Selfish Christian Hypocrites Who Don't Tip Waiters," *Daily Kos*, November 10, 2013, http://www.dailykos.com/story/2013/11/10/1254527/-MUST-SEE-Bill-Maher-BLASTS-selfish-Christian-hypocrites-who-don-t-tip-waiters#.

11. Oliver Balch, "The Relevance of Gandhi in the Capitalism Debate," *The Guardian*, January 28, 2013, http://www.theguardian.com/sustainable-business/blog/relevance-gandhi-capitalism-debate-rajni-bakshi.

12. Robert Love, "The Smart Money Is on the 50+ Crowd," *AARP The Magazine*, June/July 2014.

Chapter 5: Those to Whom We Give

1. David Leonhardt and Kevin Quealy, "The American Middle Class Is No Longer the World's Richest," *New York Times*, April 22, 2014, http://www.nytimes.com/2014/04/23/upshot/the-american-middle-class-is-no-longer-the-worlds-richest.html?abt=0002&abg=0.

2. Roger Altman, "Surprise: The Economy Isn't as Bad as You Think" *Time*, July 28, 2014, 42, http://time.com/3000991/surprise-the-economy-isnt-as-bad-as-you-think/.

3. Mark Gongloff, "45 Million Americans Still Stuck Below Poverty Line: Census," *Huffington Post*, September 16, 2014, http://www.huffingtonpost.com/2014/09/16/poverty-household-income_n_5828974.html.

4. Mark Hrywna, "Giving Estimated at $335.17 Billion for 2013," *The NonProfit Times*, June 17, 2014, http://www.thenonprofittimes.com/news-articles/giving-usa-2013/.

5. Brian Kaylor, "Church Giving Drops Even as Charitable Giving Increases," *Ethics Daily*, September 5, 2014, http://www.ethicsdaily.com/church-giving-drops-even-as-charitable-giving-increases-cms-22105.

6. "Holiday Giving Guide," Charity Navigator, accessed January 31, 2015, http://www.charitynavigator.org/index.cfm?bay=content.view&cpid=519#.VcAkfflVhBf.

7. Adam Taylor, "Chart: The World's Most Generous Countries," *Washington Post*, November 19, 2014, https://www.washingtonpost.com/news/worldviews/wp/2014/11/19/chart-the-worlds-most-generous-countries/.

8. Warren Bird, "'Red Shirt Church' Rallies to Serve Hungriest Zip Code in America," Leadership Network, October 7, 2014, http://leadnet.org/red-shirt-church-rallies-to-serve-hungriest-zip-code-in-america/.

9. "Holiday Giving Guide," Charity Navigator, accessed January 31, 2015, http://www.charitynavigator.org/index.cfm?bay=content.view&cpid=1812#.VcAliPlVhBd.

10. Mike Slaughter, *Change the World: Recovering the Message and Mission of Jesus* (Nashville: Abingdon Press, 2010), 117-23.

11. Shane Claiborne, "The Joy of Sharing," *Animate Practices DVD* (Minneapolis: Spark House, 2014).

Chapter 6: Responsible Investing

1. Charles Edward White, "What Wesley Practiced and Preached About Money," *Leadership Journal* 8, no. 1 (Winter 1987), http://www.christianitytoday.com/le/1987/winter/87l1027.html?paging=off.

2. Ibid.

3. John Wesley, *The Sermons of John Wesley*, ed. Thomas Jackson, Global Ministries of the United Methodist Church, accessed February 7, 2015,

http://www.umcmission.org/Find-Resources/John-Wesley-Sermons/Sermon-50-The-Use-of-Money.

4. Ronin, "The Berry College Campus," *Atlas Obscura*, accessed February 7, 2015, http://www.atlasobscura.com/places/the-berry-college-campus.

5. Dan Caplinger, "3 Social Security Myths Debunked," *USA Today*, October 26, 2014, http://www.usatoday.com/story/money/personalfinance/2014/10/26/three-social-security-myths-you-cant-afford-to-believe/17849183/.

6. "Fewer Families Have IRAs or 401(k) Plans," *Dayton Daily News*, November 29, 2014.

7. Bruce Kennedy, "Shocking Number of Americans Have No Retirement Savings," *CBS News*, August 18, 2014, http://www.cbsnews.com/news/shocking-number-of-americans-have-no-retirement-savings/.

8. Jonnelle Marte, "Nearly a Quarter of Fortune 500 Companies Still Offer Pensions to New Hires," *Washington Post*, September 5, 2014, http://www.washingtonpost.com/news/get-there/wp/2014/09/05/nearly-a-quarter-of-fortune-500-companies-still-offer-pensions-to-new-hires/.

9. Kennedy, "Shocking Number of Americans Have No Retirement Savings."

10. "U.S. Students So-so on Finance Test," *Dayton Daily News*, July 13, 2014, A14,

11. Ibid., A14.

12. "Evaluating Investment Risk," Standard and Poor's, Accessed February 15, 2015, http://fc.standardandpoors.com/sites/client/generic/axa/axa4/Article.vm?topic=5991&siteContent=8088#003.

13. Katherine Muniz, "20 Ways Americans Are Blowing Their Money," *USA Today*, March 24, 2014, http://www.usatoday.com/story/money/personalfinance/2014/03/24/20-ways-we-blow-our-money/6826633/.

14. "Frequently Asked Questions," The Lampo Group, Inc., accessed February 15, 2015, https://www.daveramsey.com/company/faq/#emergency_fund.

15. Virginia C. McGuire, "NerdWallet's Best Savings Accounts," NerdWallet, June 15, 2015, http://www.nerdwallet.com/blog/banking/nerdwallets-best-savings-accounts/.

16. Peggy Noonan, "'Go and Repair My House,' Heard the Saint of Assissi," *Wall Street Journal*, March 15, 2013, http://www.wsj.com/articles/SB10001424127887323393304578360853499727768.

17. Matt Krantz, "Sin Pays! Tobacco Stocks Light Up," *America's Markets*, February 24, 2015, http://americasmarkets.usatoday.com/2015/02/24/sin-pays-tobacco-lights-up-for-investors/.

18. Eric Petroff, "Change the World One Investment at a Time," *Investopedia*, accessed February 15, 2015, http://www.investopedia.com/articles/07/sri-two-styles.asp.

19. Ibid.

20. Mike Slaughter, *Change the World: Recovering the Message and Mission of Jesus* (Nashville, Abingdon Press), 15–17.

Chapter 7: Taxes and the Common Good

1. "History of Tax Resistance," *Wikipedia*, accessed March 14, 2015, https://en.wikipedia.org/wiki/History_of_tax_resistance.

2. "Who Was Lady Godiva?," *Ask History*, October 22, 2014, http://www.history.com/news/ask-history/who-was-lady-godiva.

3. Eric Foner and John A. Garraty, "Boston Tea Party," History.com, accessed March 14, 2015, http://www.history.com/topics/american-revolution/boston-tea-party.

4. "About Us," Teaparty.org, accessed March 14, 2015, http://www.teaparty.org/about-us/.

5. "Salt March," History.com, accessed March 14, 2015, http://www.history.com/topics/salt-march.

6. "Common good," Dictionary.com, 2015, http://dictionary.reference.com/browse/common+good.

7. *Catechism of the Catholic Church*, 2nd ed., http://www.scborromeo.org/ccc/p3s1c2a2.htm.

8. Jim Wallis, "Whatever Happened to the 'Common Good'?" *Time*, April 4, 2013, http://ideas.time.com/2013/04/04/whatever-happened-to-the-common-good/.

9. Joseph Jacobs and Isaac Broydé, "Tax Gatherers," *Jewish Encyclopedia*, 1906, http://www.jewishencyclopedia.com/articles/14273-tax-gatherers.

10. Christine Meléndez Ashley, "Americans Believe Government Can Do More to Combat Hunger," *breadBlog* (blog), October 30, 2014, http://blog.bread.org/2014/10/americans-believe-government-can-do-more-to-combat-hunger.html.

11. Ezra Klein, "The Budget Myth That Just Won't Die: Americans Still Think 28 Percent of the Budget Goes to Foreign Aid," *Washington Post*, November 7, 2013, http://www.washingtonpost.com/blogs/wonkblog/wp/2013/11/07/the-budget-myth-that-just-wont-die-americans-still-think-28-percent-of-the-budget-goes-to-foreign-aid/.

12. "Many Still Struggling to Get Heating Help," *Dayton Daily News*, January 2, 2015, A1, A5.

13. "BLS 2013 Sequestration Information," Bureau of Labor Statistics, March 4, 2013, http://www.bls.gov/bls/sequester_info.htm.

14. Alex Lach, "5 Facts about Overseas Outsourcing," Center for American Progress, July 9, 2012, https://www.americanprogress.org/issues/labor/news/2012/07/09/11898/5-facts-about-overseas-outsourcing/.

15. Chris Stewart and Randy Tucker, "Skills Gap Focus on College Plan," *Dayton Daily News*, January 25, 2015, A1, A10.

16. Jeremy P. Kelley and Jackie Borchardt, "Scores Show Income Gap," *Dayton Daily News*, September 17, 2013, A1, A8.

17. Ashley Halsey III, "U.S. Infrastructure Gets D+ in Annual Report," *Washington Post*, March 19, 2013, http://www.washingtonpost.com/local/trafficandcommuting/us-infrastructure-gets-d-in-annual-report/2013/03/19/c48cb010-900b-11e2-9cfd-36d6c9b5d7ad_story.html.

18. Hope Yen, "Regulators to Target Payday Loans," *Dayton Daily News*, February 2, 2015, A4.

19. David Beckmann, *Exodus from Hunger*, (Louisville, KY: Westminster John Knox Press, 2010), 134–35.

20. John Wesley, *The Sermons of John Wesley*, ed. Thomas Jackson, Global Ministries of the United Methodist Church, accessed March 21, 2015, http://www.umcmission.org/Find-Resources/John-Wesley-Sermons/Sermon-50-The-Use-of-Money.

21. "America's Sewage System and the Price of Optimism," *Time*, August 1, 1969, http://content.time.com/time/magazine/article/0,9171,901182,00.html.

Chapter 8: Work to Live or Live to Work

1. *Fast Company*, "Find Your Mission," November 2014, 67, http://www.fastcompany.com/3036585/generation-flux/i-like-to-employ-the-power-of-no-jared-leto.

2. Mike Slaughter, *Dare to Dream: Creating a God-Sized Mission Statement for Your Life* (Nashville: Abingdon Press, 2013), 16.

3. Bruce Wilkinson, *The Prayer of Jabez* (Colorado Springs: Multnomah), 2000.

4. Kathleen Sebelius, "Annual Update of the HHS Poverty Guidelines," (press release, Health and Human Services, January 22, 2014), https://www.federalregister.gov/articles/2014/01/22/2014-01303/annual-update-of-the-hhs-poverty-guidelines#t-1.

5. "State & County QuickFacts," (press release, United States Census Bureau, June 8, 2015), http://quickfacts.census.gov/qfd/states/00000.html.

6. Allison Linn, "Here's How Much Americans Think Families Need to Get By," *Today Money*, Tuesday, May 21, 2013, http://www.today.com/money/heres-how-much-americans-think-families-need-get-6C10010274.

7. Lydia Saad, "Americans Say Family of Four Needs Nearly $60K to 'Get By,'" Gallup, May 17, 2013, http://www.gallup.com/poll/162587/americans-say-family-four-needs-nearly-60k.aspx.

8. Linn, "Here's How Much Americans Think Families Need to Get By."

9. Alden Wicker, "The Salary That Will Make You Happy (Hint: It's Less than $75,000)," *Forbes*, April 24, 2012, http://www.forbes.com/sites/learnvest/2012/04/24/the-salary-that-will-make-you-happy-hint-its-less-than-75000/.

10. Gabrielle Karol, "How to Cure Your Money Comparisonitis," *LearnVest*, January 11, 2012, http://www.learnvest.com/2012/01/how-to-cure-your-money-comparisonitis/.

11. "State of the American Workplace—Employee Engagement Insights for U.S. Business Leaders," Gallup, 2013, 9, http://www.gallup.com/services/178514/state-american-workplace.aspx?utm_source=state%20of%20the%20american%20workplace&utm_medium=search&utm_campaign=tiles.

12. David Wallis, "Saving the World as a Second Career," *AARP The Magazine*, October/November 2014, 41.

Chapter 9: Choosing Our Neighbors

1. Peter Lovenheim, "How Well Do You Know Your Neighbors?" *Washington Post*, May 10, 2013, https://www.washingtonpost.com/opinions/how-well-do-you-know-your-neighbors/2013/05/10/1d1488da-b824-11e2-92f3-f291801936b8_story.html.

2. Brian Bethune, "The End of Neighbours," *Maclean's*, August 8, 2014, http://www.macleans.ca/society/the-end-of-neighbours/.

3. Lovenheim, "How Well Do You Know Your Neighbors?"

4. Jessica Olien, "Loneliness Is Deadly," *Slate*, August 23, 2013, http://www.slate.com/articles/health_and_science/medical_examiner/2013/08/dangers_of_loneliness_social_isolation_is_deadlier_than_obesity.html.

5. "Frequently Asked Questions," United States Census Bureau, accessed April 4, 2015, https://ask.census.gov/faq.php?id=5000&faqId=5971.

6. Jonathan Vespa, Jamie M. Lewis, and Rose M. Kreider, "America's Families and Living Arrangements: 2012," United States Census Bureau, August 2013, https://www.census.gov/prod/2013pubs/p20-570.pdf.

7. Claire Cain Miller, "Where Young College Graduates Are Choosing to Live," *New York Times*, October 20, 2014, http://www.nytimes.com/2014/10/20/upshot/where-young-college-graduates-are-choosing-to-live.html?_r=1&abt=0002&abg=1.

8. Jed Kolko, "Urban Headwinds, Suburban Tailwinds," Trulia, January 22, 2015, http://www.trulia.com/trends/2015/01/cities-vs-suburbs-jan-2015/.

9. Ari Weisbard, "Two Couples, One Mortgage," *The Atlantic*, July 11, 2014, http://www.theatlantic.com/business/archive/2014/07/two-couples-one-mortgage/374102/.

10. "Political Polarization in the American Public," Pew Research Center, June 12, 2014, http://www.people-press.org/2014/06/12/political-polarization-in-the-american-public/.

11. Drew Desilver, "How the Most Ideologically Polarized Americans Live Different Lives," Pew Research Center, June 13, 2014, http://www.pewresearch.org/fact-tank/2014/06/13/big-houses-art-museums-and-in-laws-how-the-most-ideologically-polarized-americans-live-different-lives/.

12. Tanzine Vega, "Wealth Gap Widens as Net Worths Drop," *Dayton Daily News*, December 13, 2014, A4.

13. "Upward Mobility Is Ranked," *Dayton Daily News*, September 7, 2013, A4.

14. Emily Badger, "The Terrible Loneliness of Growing Up Poor in Robert Putnam's America," *Washington Post*, March 6, 2015, http://www.washingtonpost.com/news/wonkblog/wp/2015/03/06/the-terrible-loneliness-of-growing-up-poor-in-robert-putnams-america/.

15. Lisa Miller, "The Money-Empathy Gap," *New York Magazine*, July 1, 2012, http://nymag.com/news/features/money-brain-2012-7/.

16. Scott Christian, "The Problem with Creating 'Christian' Versions of Things," Ministry Matters, April 10, 2015, http://www.ministrymatters.com/all/entry/5955/the-problem-with-creating-christian-versions-of-thing.

17. Michael Lipka, "Many U.S. Congregations Are Still Racially Segregated, but Things Are Changing," Pew Research Center, December 8, 2014, http://www.pewresearch.org/fact-tank/2014/12/08/many-u-s-congregations-are-still-racially-segregated-but-things-are-changing-2/

18. Bob Smietana, "Sunday Morning America Still Segregated–and That's OK with Worshipers," LifeWay Research, January 15, 2015, http://www.lifewayresearch.com/2015/01/15/sunday-morning-in-america-still-segregated-and-thats-ok-with-worshipers/.

19. Mike Slaughter, *Renegade Gospel: Rebel Jesus* (Nashville: Abingdon Press, 2014), 28.

20. Shane Claiborne, *The Irresistible Revolution: Living as an Ordinary Radical* (Grand Rapids, MI: Zondervan, 2006), 70.

21. David Brooks, "To Succeed at Life, People Have to Be in the Ballgame," *Dayton Daily News*, July 14, 2014.

22. *Happy*. DVD, directed by Roko Belic (Los Angeles, California: Wadi Rum Productions, 2011).

Chapter 10: The Joy of Simplicity

1. Carolyn Gregoire, "The Psychology of Materialism: Why It's Making You Unhappy," *Huffington Post*, December 15, 2103, updated January 23, 2014, http://www.huffingtonpost.com/2013/12/15/psychology-materialism_n_4425982.html?.

2. Rik Pieters, "Bidirectional Dynamics of Materialism and Loneliness: Not Just a Vicious Cycle," *Journal of Consumer Research* 40, no. 4 (December 2013): 615-31, http://www.jstor.org/stable/10.1086/671564?seq=1#page_scan_tab_contents.

3. "Why Is Everyone So Busy?," *Economist*, December 20, 2014, http://www.economist.com/news/christmas-specials/21636612-time-poverty-problem-partly-perception-and-partly-distribution-why.

4. Shea Bennet, "This Is How Much Time We Spend on Social Networks Every Day," *Social Times*, November 18, 2014, http://www.adweek.com/socialtimes/social-media-minutes-day/503160.

5. "11 Facts About American Eating Habits," DoSomething.org, accessed April 11, 2015, https://www.dosomething.org/facts/11-facts-about-american-eating-habits.

6. Rachel Tepper, "In First, Americans Spent More in Restaurants Than Grocery Stores," *Yahoo! Food*, March 6, 2015, https://www.yahoo.com/food/in-first-americans-spent-more-in-restaurants-than-112803758886.html.

7. Richard Foster, *Freedom of Simplicity* (San Francisco: HarperSanFrancisco, 1981), 32.

8. "House Hunters – IMDb," *The Internet Movie Database (IMDb)*, accessed April 11, 2015, http://www.imdb.com/title/tt0369117/?ref_=nv_sr_1.

9. Foster, *Freedom of Simplicity*, 18.

10. Ibid., 49.

11. Lauren Dalessandro, "Should Christians Be Rich?," *Relevant Magazine*, May 9, 2013, http://www.relevantmagazine.com/life/should-christians-be-rich.

12. "Tiny House Nation – IMDb," *The Internet Movie Database (IMDb)*, accessed April 11, 2015, http://www.imdb.com/title/tt3869500/?ref_=fn_al_tt_1.

13. Michael Salguero, "The Tiny House Movement," *Huffington Post*, September 12, 2014, http://www.huffingtonpost.com/mike-salguero/the-tiny-house-movement_b_5811058.html.

14. Kathy Gottberg, "10 Commandments for a Smart and Simple Life," *Huffington Post*, May 26, 2015, http://www.huffingtonpost.com/kathy-gottberg/10-commandments-for-a-smart-and-simple-life_b_6906260.html.

15. Anna Medaris Miller, "The Health Benefits of Simple Living," *U.S. News*, November 5, 2014, http://health.usnews.com/health-news/health-wellness/articles/2014/11/05/the-health-benefits-of-simple-living.

16. StanCorp Financial Group, Inc., "The Frugal Habits of Millionaires," in *Mainspring Minute*, Summer 2014.

Epilogue

1. Mark and Lisa Scandrette, *FREE—Spending Your Time and Money on What Matters Most* (Downers Grove, IL: IVP Books, 2013), 23–24.